OUT HERE

OUT HERE

Wisdom from the Wilderness

By Carolyn Highland

For information on purchasing bulk quantities of this book, or to
obtain media excerpts or invite the author to speak at an event,
please visit rmbooks.com and select the "Contact" tab.

RMB | Rocky Mountain Books Ltd.
rmbooks.com
@rmbooks
facebook.com/rmbooks

Cataloguing data available from Library and Archives Canada
ISBN 9781771604499 (paperback)
ISBN 9781771604505 (electronic)

Cover photo © Lumina / Stocksy United

Printed and bound in Canada

We would like to also take this opportunity to acknowledge the traditional
territories upon which we live and work. In Calgary, Alberta, we acknowledge
the Niitsítapi (Blackfoot) and the people of the Treaty 7 region in Southern
Alberta, which includes the Siksika, the Piikuni, the Kainai, the Tsuut'ina and
the Stoney Nakoda First Nations, including Chiniki, Bearpaw, and Wesley First
Nations. The City of Calgary is also home to Métis Nation of Alberta, Region
III. In Victoria, British Columbia, we acknowledge the traditional territories
of the Lkwungen (Esquimalt, and Songhees), Malahat, Pacheedaht, Scia'new,
T'Sou-ke and W̱SÁNEĆ (Pauquachin, Tsartlip, Tsawout, Tseycum) peoples.

We acknowledge the financial support of the Government of Canada
through the Canada Book Fund and the Canada Council for the
Arts, and of the province of British Columbia through the British
Columbia Arts Council and the Book Publishing Tax Credit.

For my parents, who never told me to
pursue something more practical.

For all of the young people who are fostering a big
dream in their hearts it may take years to realize.

For all the past versions of myself who fearlessly walked
the steep, winding trail to get here. We made it.

Contents

Out Here

Wilderness equalizes us. It sets us all on flat even ground. We are all small in the face of mountains, all vulnerable before swelling seas, all dwarfed by the limitless sky. Facing the elements, we are our raw, basic selves. All else falls away. In that rawness there is clarity – all the wind on the water going still so we can see straight into the depths.

We are no longer defined by the years we have lived, or what we have been called, or the things we can do. We are all equally alive, swaying in the arms of the ancient earth. We are all equally young next to the rocks and the waves.

With us we have only the parts of ourselves we can carry, only what travels with us always. We may find things that have been hidden, we may remember what we had allowed ourselves to forget. We may stretch ourselves taller and wider to mimic towering trees, taller and wider than we ever imagined.

Back where we're from the land is covered. Cloaked in artifice, pounded and blasted and moved and molded to our convenience. Back where we're from we are covered. Steeped in beliefs that belong to others, folded over and compressed and colored until we forget the feel of our own skin. Out here the grass grows long, the trees stretch tall, our eyes open wide.

Where we're from we are so often looking down. Down at the things we hold in our hands, down at our own feet as we walk, down when we can't meet someone else's eyes.

Being out here calls you to look in all directions at once. Down, at the plants and animals you walk beside; out, at all that lies between you and the horizon; up, at the sun and the clouds and the big ancient blue above us; and in, at the tiny reflection of the universe we hold within our ribs, behind our eyes, in our fingers and ears and mouths and toes. Our eyes no longer squint, trained on abstract things we hold in our hands, they open and clear to take in all that is around us.

Where we're from we're kings and queens of concrete, we cradle the power in our hands. Returning to the wild we are reminded that all we have created are constructs, all control conjured up in our minds. Out here we do not have to go to churches and temples to pray to the idea of something greater, we can simply stand before mountains and see it.

Being out here makes you feel small in ways you need to feel small. We are not all-important, we are not all knowing, we are not invincible. We are blades of grass, we are particles of wind, we are stones smoothed by water. Think of all the trillions of things happening each second all over this planet, the breathing, the flowing, the moving, the growing, the loving, the living, the dying, and try to feel like you are all that matters. You cannot.

Being out here makes you feel big in ways you need to feel big. We are not a set of nine numbers, we are not a one-word definition, we are not contained. There are mountains and seas and skies within us. Try to think of all the shades of yourself, of everything you've ever seen or thought or dreamed or felt or believed, and try not to feel infinite. You cannot.

Being out in the wild reminds us of all the smallness and largeness of ourselves because this earth, this sea and sky and rock and tree and mountain, this is where we are from. Not a town with a name and a sign, but the ancient, persisting, elemental earth. We are not names and birthdates but hearts and souls reflecting the browns, the blues, the greens.

Waking Up in the Wilderness

I woke in the middle of the night to cold on my nose and a black strip of sky smattered with stars in my vision. It was all I could see, my sleeping bag cinched up around my face, laid out on the bare ground. I lay there unmoving, every cell of my body awake and aware of itself. It felt as though I'd been tapped on the shoulder, as though some massive universal force had tugged at me, whispering, "you need to see this."

I'd spent the few days prior hiking through tussock and scree and contemplating the uncertainty of my future. In less than a week my semester in New Zealand would be over and I would find myself yet again a recent college graduate without a plan. The mountain air had been whirring with questions I didn't have answers to yet, like where I'd live and what I'd do and whom I'd be with. Would I choose the easy, comfortable route and try to find a job in a city I didn't really want to live in because my friends were there? Would I choose a route that was less challenging but safer? Or would I do something entirely different, something that I felt in my heart but would require me striking out alone? Out here, I woke up every day with a purpose – with the pure and yet complex purpose of picking up my home and walking to where I would place it next. Back in the frontcountry, the questions and options tumbled and spun and made me dizzy.

When two of my expedition mates tried to convince me to sleep outside on the night of Thanksgiving, one of our last in the backcountry, I declined, citing my exhaustion and desire to get a good night's sleep. I liked the idea of sleeping outside better than the actuality of it, especially at high altitude in mid-spring. I would inevitably toss and turn in the cold and wake up to sand flies biting my face. I wanted the comfort of the inside of the only house we had out here. But before I even entered the tent I felt called back outside, felt called to sleep beside my two best friends underneath the sky.

Instead of feeling irritated when I awoke, I was seized by the feeling that more than ever I was exactly where I needed to be in that moment in my life. I was suddenly calm. It was all simple; it was all right before me. It was all embodied by what I was doing in that exact moment, by the choice I had made that night, a choice that seemed so insignificant at the time but that I realized then actually represented everything I was about to do, everything I wanted my life to be.

In the tent, I would have had a warm, pleasant, uninterrupted night's sleep. I would have been comfortable. It would have been easy. It was my initial reaction because it was the path of least resistance; it was the choice that felt like the best one because it was the easiest. But it wasn't. The best choice was to drag my sleeping bag out into the chilly night air and lay it beside two people who brought out in me what I wanted to be brought out. And so I knew it would have to be, and would be for the rest of my life.

There wasn't a sense of obligation or pressure, it was just clear that it was the right choice and it was the one I would make. I wouldn't spend my life living easily. I would live a certain way, I would surround myself with certain people. Being in New Zealand had awoken me to exactly the way I wanted to live my life. Not in a literal sense – I was not planning on spending the rest of my days in the backcountry. But in a sense of the way I felt when I was out there, in the way I acted, in the way I was. In the way I inhabited my real self so fully and completely. In the way I spent time with people who made me better. Who made me more of who I was.

And I knew in that moment as I gazed up at the stars, my nose frozen from the air but my arms warm from my friends on either side of me, that this is the path I would follow for the rest of my life. This is what I would do. This is the way I would live. I would travel uphill and jump into cold water and be kind and supportive and goofy and real. I would do what felt right in the deepest and purest part of me, even when it was difficult. I didn't know yet what it would look like, but I knew what it would feel like. It wasn't even a choice, it just was. This is the answer, it whispered. This is the way. It was right before me, as clear as the night sky above our heads.

Years after I took my last steps out of the New Zealand back-country, I find myself thousands of miles from home on the other side of the US, having heeded the pull of the southern hemisphere stars. I find myself living the life I'd imagined. One that looks different from anything I ever could have dreamed up but feels precisely the way I knew it needed to. It was a difficult and confusing and exhausting and long and windy trail to get here, but it was the right one. And I am a fuller and richer and happier version of myself for it.

How incredible it is to – through your presence in this grand vast environment – connect with something that lies so deep within your own soul. And that is the proof, I think, that everything in this universe is connected to every other thing. That by placing my feet on the mountains and my hands into the speargrass and my ass onto the slushy snow and my head on the tussock, I was actually connecting, little by little, with myself. With something inside me long before I ever set foot in New Zealand but called to the surface by its long-lost relatives. By the sky and the stones and the streams and the snow and the stars. A message that could only be heard outside.

That is the gift wilderness gives us. It reminds us of who we are and pushes us to be that. You were always there, it whispers, but it provides us with the clear reflecting glass to see it. This is who you are, it tells us. This is who we are.

Strength

I still remember the feeling of spring-loaded energy as I rounded the curve in my first 200-meter dash in the first grade, flinging myself through the bend and powering through the straight-away to the finish. I felt propelled by something deep within, from an energy source that seemed to have just been awakened. Suddenly I was flying down the track, an unstoppable momentum in my legs. I crossed the line spent, feeling the heat of exertion in my lungs, but also a distinct sense of power, of strength.

It was a first taste of pushing my body, of the siren call of doing something difficult. I continued to feel the draw, through Nordic ski races in high school, road half-marathons in college, trail ultras and long-distance ski mountaineering races in my 20s.

There was something strangely magnetic about it – to do something I wasn't sure if I could, something that seemed crazy. I consistently felt myself drawn to opportunities to prove myself, to move faster and farther and longer than I had before, than other people could or wanted to.

And with each hit of adrenaline, with each successful completion of a difficult endeavor, it became less of something I did and more of who I was. I was a person who ran and skied and hiked for hours through the mountains. I felt the most like myself when I was sweating and breathing hard and moving forward.

In order to do all of these things, thousands of tiny pieces of your body must work together in a certain way. Bones and muscles and ligaments must perform a synchronized, choreographed dance that allows you to move the way you want to. When your body is functioning properly, it is easy to forget this. When your body is functioning properly, you just run. You just ski. You just move. It is only when something goes wrong that you become acutely aware of the impact of any one of those parts on the overall performance of the whole, on your ability to do the things you love.

* * *

I felt it instantly, the movement that shouldn't have happened. The grass was wet and as I went to plant all my weight on my left foot, I felt my knee extend forward past where a knee is supposed to extend. There was no pain, no pop, just a certain knowing that something had happened I couldn't undo, that there would suddenly be a distinct before this moment and after this moment.

The panic pulsed through me in an instant, radiating out to all my extremities, to all the dark corners of my mind. So many things suddenly seemed to hang in the balance. What if it was my ACL? What if I couldn't run? What if I couldn't ski?

You start to reason with yourself, to think maybe if you just shake it out a little, it'll be fine, that it was just one bad movement, akin to a minor ankle roll, and you'll ice it for a day and then laugh it off. That there's no way you could have possibly done real damage to your knee while playing a game called birdie on a perch.

You start to bargain with the universe. You'll never play ridiculous games in wet grass again that put what you love in jeopardy. You'll stop basing so much of your happiness on your body's ability to function at a high level – but if it's cool, you'd really love to not be injured so you can continue to experience the happiness that's based on your body's ability to function at a high level.

The lessons we adamantly insist we don't need to learn, the ones we resist from our core, are the ones the universe is mostly like to push toward us anyway with its eyebrows raised. Like hell you don't need to learn this.

* * *

A few weeks after I slipped on the grass, I was slated to spend two weeks backpacking on the Colorado Trail. We'd spent months planning and organizing and looking at topos and dehydrating food, and I was going to slap a brace on my knee and be fine. The first stage of grief is denial.

With me were two other women – Jules, a childhood friend from Maine, and Jess, a trail running buddy from Denver. We set up our first camp on a pass next to the trailhead, and I lay awake in my sleeping bag for hours, an internal battle raging in my mind and keeping me from sleep. I wanted to go back to the moment I jumped off the wet grass and undo it, I wanted to believe I could backpack for two weeks and be fine, I wanted to know if what I was about to do was reckless and foolish. Running through me was the panic that had entered my body the moment I felt my knee hyperextend. It came in and out, stronger in some moments than others, but it was always present. What if I had to stop doing what I loved?

When we set out the next morning for our first day on the trail, I felt hyperaware of my body as it moved. Hiking and running are these beautiful, rhythmic activities that bring your body back to a primal state, a forward motion that feels instinctive and organic. But now I couldn't surrender to the dance because something was off. One dancer wasn't following the choreography, and it took me out of the flow, out of the moment.

The mountains had always been a place where I felt like myself, where I dialed into an inner stillness and outer rhythm that felt absolutely essential. But now, moving more slowly and with less confidence, the connection seemed to deteriorate. I wanted to move the way I was used to, the way I knew I could.

And so, when I wasn't able to tap into my inner zen wilderness princess, I became cranky and frustrated and snapped at my friends. The second stage of grief is anger.

Pain is inevitable, but suffering is optional. Suffering is ultimately created by a resistance to what is, by a sense that the universe owed you something different than what you got, that things were supposed to be a different way.

If we don't like what is, we have two productive options: to try our best to be still with it, to accept it, or to take forward action in the ways we can. Passive complaining or wishing things were different are fruitless, addictive options that make us miserable to be around and create a challenging situation that is more unpleasant than it has to be.

A few days in, Jules let us know she was experiencing Achilles pain. She told us this calmly, as a mere statement of what was. We moved some weight around in packs to allow her body a break, she hiked at the back of the pack to be able to take more deliberate steps and treated her feet to a 15-minute creek or alpine lake soak every night after dinner.

Her pain didn't change her disposition; it didn't seem to interfere with her experience of being out in the wilderness for an extended period of time. It was simply another fact of reality. She didn't ignore the situation, but she didn't dwell in it either. She accepted it and took the steps in her power to improve it.

One night Jules and I sat down near a creek in a lush valley after our longest day yet. We had set out in the morning with the intention of hiking 16 miles to a campsite mentioned in the guidebook, but we found it already occupied upon arrival and had to continue on to an area with "potential campsites" in a zone that would add anywhere from one to three miles to the day's total. I had already been in a bad mood prior to the realization that we would have to continue, frustrated I wasn't able to crush ascents the way I usually did, and experiencing a twinge in my back from carrying an extra heavy pack to displace the weight for Jules. The three of us had gotten into a pointless passive-aggressive snap-off about where we should stop to get water and were exhausted by the time we finally found a campable spot in a lush valley near a creek.

Jules had been soaking her feet nightly for a few days now, but after peeling off my socks and realizing my toe blisters were steadily worsening, I decided to join her. The water was snowmelt flowing down from high above us, and the evening was cold enough to be bundled up in a puffy and wool beanie. I balled my socks up on the grass next to me, rolled up my fleece pants and stuck my foot in, and almost instantly yanked it back out and shook it off. I had no problem putting my entire body into cold water for a few seconds, but once the icy burn penetrated my skin, every cell in my body screamed for it to be over. If it were a little less cold, I would soak.

I watched in awe as Jules stepped into the creek with both feet, Chacos still on, set the timer on her watch, and stood. She was still the entire time, never taking her feet out of the water or even adjusting their position. She chatted and admired the scenery, and when the timer on her watch went off, she stepped out of the creek.

The cold was just what was, was just a fact of reality she had to contend with. But despite the inevitable discomfort of the temperature, the water was what her body needed, and so she stood still. She took the forward action she was able to, allowing the pain without giving in to suffering.

The stillness was the problem. My body craved motion. It didn't want to stand in the creek for 15 minutes, it wanted to jump in the lake and run back out. It was the same reason I'd rather run for five hours than do yoga for five minutes. The idea of my body being still, of not being able to move in all the ways that brought me joy, caused a whirring panic in my mind. The threat of outer stillness was creating a lack of inner stillness. And the only way to accept one was to achieve the other.

* * *

During the winter of my freshman year of high school, I walked into dinner at the lodge we were staying at for the Nordic skiing state championships and was stopped by a popular senior and congratulated on my race the day before. She had done so in front of a table of other seniors, who smiled at me and nodded in confirmation that what I had done was, in fact, badass. I was 15 years old and had never even spoken to these seniors, so far above me in status and social ease that they felt like celebrities.

The day before had been the high school Class B Maine state championship skate skiing race, a 5k at a tiny resort called Black Mountain. I'd been skiing well all season, scoring for the team (meaning I was one of the top four), but the state skate race had been different. I'd unleashed something previously unseen, tapped into some sort of bottomless drive to perform that had slashed my mile splits by minutes. I soared through the finish, completely worked, leaning on my ski poles in the finish area with my chest heaving, leaning over and hanging my head to catch my breath. I heard them announce my name in the top ten of all female racers for the day, and heard the message coming from somewhere deep inside me: you are strong and that is good.

I placed ninth in the state that day, helping lead my team to an overall victory, and spent the rest of the weekend basking in the pleasant surprise, the impressed praise – a freshman had placed top ten. And suddenly this feeling, of doing something unexpected, of surpassing people's expectations, floated up in front of me, beckoning. The synapses in my brain started creating a path, a path that would become as well worn and familiar as the trails behind my house. Being strong, stronger than other people thought you could be, meant that seniors stopped you on your way to the salad bar for high fives and your coaches beamed at you and other teams knew your name. It meant you were perceived as worthy. It meant you perceived yourself as worthy. Regardless of the pursuit, the circumstances, the activity, it boiled down to an equation: strength = worthiness.

I kept chasing opportunities to prove myself, craving more and more each time. In college I started running road half-marathons, training in the soupy Midwest heat and trying to dial down my mile splits. By my mid-20s, I was ready for something grittier, and switched exclusively to trails, running ultramarathons, 30ks, 25ks and any long trail race I could get my hands on.

But what I found was that the initial hit of goodness, the chest balloon of pride, became slightly deflated if I didn't keep upping the ante. Once I had run a certain distance, it didn't feel as good to run it again. I had arrived already knowing I was capable of achieving my goal, and so its achievement felt perfunctory. I found myself compelled to keep seeking out bigger and bigger challenges to attain the same results.

When I was 25, I finished my first ultra with tears of joy streaming down my face. I had run 36 miles in the Grand Canyon over a period of nine hours, and was so shocked and amazed that I rounded the last curve of the course and was crying before I even realized what was happening. It was the most jacked-up version of the strength = worthiness high I had ever experienced. I felt proud of what I had done and who I was. In my mind, what I was experiencing was a direct product of having run 36 miles. Running ultras feels good. But what it was, perhaps even more than that, was that loving myself feels good.

And so the neural pathways became worn with a message that was confusing process with outcome. I began to equate the vehicle that was bringing me the feeling with the feeling itself, not realizing they were, in fact, completely separate entities. I was chasing an incorrectly identified feeling, something I'd mislabeled. It wasn't the sugar, it was the sweetness. It wasn't the sunshine, it was the warmth. It wasn't the instruments, it was the melody. And though I didn't know it yet, there were many ways to skin that cat.

* * *

Toward the end of our hike on the Colorado Trail, the thunderstorms started hitting in the morning and I felt a twinge in my Achilles. We arrived at our camp at an alpine lake at 11:30

a.m. and spent the following 15 hours in the tent waiting out a storm that never subsided. I'd felt the twinge on the final downhill mile of the day, trying to get to the lake quickly so I could jump into it naked before the party behind us caught up. A sharp, shooting pain that made me wince and stop in my tracks. Not now. Not when I'd managed things with my knee to the point where I was able to hike nearly 20 miles a day and not feel it. I felt myself being pulled down the panic spiral once again, going down the darkest roads this could potentially lead to.

I rolled it out on my Nalgene after a few hours in the tent, and we discussed strategy for the remaining two days on the trail. We were starting to slowly lose our minds in the tent, whether that meant actually being able to read *The Goldfinch* in its entirety or taking four-hour naps out of sheer boredom, so we needed to make a plan. It got thrown out originally as a crazy idea that started to seem less crazy as time passed and the lightning remained within a few miles' radius of our tent.

We had ten- and 13-mile days slated to finish out our trip, taking us into Durango in two days' time. What if we just woke up really early and tried to do it all at once? In full health, I would have reveled in the idea of a 23-mile day with full weight. But now, with the future of my knee's condition still uncertain and the added wildcard of a stressed-out Achilles, I was nervous to try to push it. I found myself frustrated yet again, wishing my body would just be instantly restored to its former glory. Twenty-three miles in any other circumstance would not have been something I would have blinked my eyes at, and now I had to consider whether or not it was wise or even possible.

Ultimately, we decided we would go for an alpine start and try to make it all the way out of the backcountry to the CT's southern terminus in Durango the next day. I again lay awake in my sleeping bag, resisting the situation with all of my heart. I felt not a single shred of compassion or understanding or kindness for my body, only anger and trepidation. I lay there and wished with all my might that I were different.

In the blackness we packed up camp and followed the trail into the cold fog. I took careful steps, trying not to upset my Achilles, and tried to accept my position at the back of the pack, not one I took in stride. I hated being at the back, hated feeling like I wasn't capable of leading the pack. I wanted to be strong, wanted to be out ahead, charging up hills and cruising through flats and ballet dancing my way down descents.

The day required much more focus and patience from me than it normally would have. I had to think about my foot placement and my movements far more than I usually did, not able to access the smooth-flow state I craved when my body was working properly. And in the slowness of my movements, I began to think about strength.

To me, strength had always had to do with how my body felt. If I was moving fast and feeling healthy and able to do things that were difficult, I was strong. Right now, having to baby my body and move slowly and more deliberately, I felt weak.

But what I realized, as the sun came up and the miles dragged on and we inched ever closer to our destination, injury or no, was that strength manifests in innumerable ways, not just the one I had always ascribed to. Strength for me today would not mean I was out in front crushing miles, it would not mean my body was functioning like a well-oiled machine, it would not mean I did something difficult without having to try that hard.

Strength for me today would mean I started from where I was, not from where I wished I was or wanted to be, and moved forward. Strength would mean feeling weak and continuing anyway. Strength would mean trying to allow my body to show up in whatever way it was going to show up, and working from there. It would mean coming from a place of love and not a place of fear, it would mean being big and magnanimous and brave. It would mean changing everything I thought I knew about being strong.

We reached the parking lot late that afternoon, and ceremoniously threw our backpacks off our shoulders. We had done it. We had arrived.

I felt like absolute shit. My Achilles ached, my knee felt as wobbly and unstable as ever and, among the civilized again, I finally began to smell the two weeks of sweat and dirt covering my body and all of my belongings.

I sat down on the curb of the lot. I had done it. It hadn't felt good, but I'd done it. I breathed out. Maybe, just maybe, hiking 23 miles slowly when I was injured actually required more strength than doing it quickly in full health. And even though I didn't fully believe it yet, and wouldn't for some time, I allowed myself to feel a little bit strong.

It is far simpler to love our bodies when they are working for us, when they are healthy and strong and powerful. It's easy to fall into the trap of wishing we had bionic joints or tireless muscles or were in the same shape we were when we were training for something big. But just as we expect our people to keep showing up with love for us when we're down or sick or sad or broken, we must also show up for ourselves and our bodies in the same way. Love your body even when it isn't working the way you want it to, even when you're frustrated. Say to it what you would want someone to say to you, that you're in this together and you'll get through it. Love your body in sickness and in health, in brokenness and in strength, and all the places in between.

What Would You Do with Your Days?

Breathe in fresh air for as many hours as possible. Wake up for sunrise. Ski. Run. Hike. Backpack. Kayak. Sleep in a tent. Explore. Be with friends. Drink IPAS. Listen to music. Dance. Write. Make big dinners with people I love. Travel. Learn how to climb. Learn how to play an instrument. Learn how to drive stick. Take lots of pictures. Spend time with my family. Go on adventures with my dog. Sit on decks and porches for hours at a time. Pile a bunch of friends in the car and drive somewhere awesome. Drink in the sunshine. Catch snowflakes on my tongue. Smile so hard my jaw hurts and my eyes close involuntarily.

Bake bread. Sing. Wear overalls. Keep my phone on airplane mode. Be honest. Create. Love. Be appreciative. Say it out loud. Meditate. Read books in comfy chairs. Snuggle. Laugh until my jaw hurts and my stomach cramps up. Wear fleece. Look at the stars. Climb mountains. Drive to new places. Get rosy cheeks. Wear beanies. Feel the tired warmth in the car on the way home after a day outside. Make someone's day better.

Experience the particular humor of children. Breathe fresh air. Braid my hair. Be as goofy as possible. Skip. Embody the boundless spirit of those who have left us too soon. Practice loving kindness.

Go fast and slow where it's appropriate. Have long talks. Pick wild blueberries. Make people laugh. Cook on my camp stove. Make a fire. Sit around that fire with my favorite people and drink good beer. Wear mittens. Wear Chacos. Wear Smartwool socks. Wear those last two at the same time and look super cool doing it. Put on lotion that smells good. Listen to wind rustle leaves. Play in the snow. Lose myself in the moment. Do things that scare me. Break a sweat. Route find. Give great hugs. Trust the universe. Persevere. Fall down and have a sense of humor about it. Let the gladness spill out.

Feel and express gratitude. Smile when my alarm goes off because I know it's for a good reason. Have a picnic. Listen to live music outside. Speak Chilean Spanish. Appreciate the moment while it's happening. Go uphill and downhill. Not think about how I look. Write in my journal. Reflect. Spend time alone in nature. Get to a great view and sit there way too long because I can't pull myself away. Help other people. Sit on the ground. Eat food that makes my body feel good.

Watch the mountains turn from golden blue to smoky purple to shadowy charcoal and love every stage for its particular beauty. Be able to pull each item in my backpack out based on feel alone. Knead dough and let it be a therapeutic experi-ence. Pull over to look at the view. Pee outside. Catch both 11:11s. Jump in alpine lakes and let the cold freshness wake up every cell in my body. Do things that make most other people say, "She's crazy." Chase runner's and hiker's and skier's highs. Go on hut trips. Make people feel good about themselves. Do things that challenge me. Sit on the dock. Lay in an inner tube upside down and look out at the lake. Waterski. Take long walks. Climb trees.

Make someone else's day. Be optimistic and hopeful. Do what feels right. Reach for things. Not look away. Make new friends. Rack up scrapes and bruises. Use my spork and Nalgene and thermos instead of disposable versions of those things. Drink peppermint hot chocolate. Communicate openly and honestly. Be generous. Fly, even for a few seconds. Longboard on a wide, flat, open road. Check things off my to-do list. Feel the happi-ness well up in my chest.

Tell all the people in my life how amazing I think they are. Cry because I'm happy. Dangle my arm out the car win-dow. Feel good about myself. Do things I didn't think I could. Dream about the future and do the work in the present. Be still. Feel glad I am a human alive in the universe. Yell "My heart hurts!" as I look at the beautiful things around me. Lean in.

Know Before You Go

It was a warm, sunny March day in the Indian Peaks Wilderness, and we dug the pit even though we didn't have to. We got our shovels and probes and he showed me how to measure the dimensions, and then we dug out enough snow so we could both stand in the pit. We smoothed the walls and he took out his crystal card and snow saw and paracord and other tools that would help us perform snow tests to analyze the snowpack.

Were there weak layers? Where were they? How much force would it take to cause one to fail? He showed me how to do a shear test and an extended column test and how to categorize different types of snow crystals under the magnifying glass.

We toured an easy four miles up into a snowy basin, and turned around without getting into anything above a 30-degree angle. We enjoyed some mellow turns in an open meadow before descending back below treeline, ready for a slow cruise to the parking lot.

"We" was me and him, the snow hydrologist. The first person to make me feel like I was *it*, like the wait was over.

We had met in the parking lot of the mountain we both skied at, on an ordinary gray day in January. I'd been crouched on the ground next to my car, trying to light my camp stove and struggling with a clogged fuel line when he and his friend came over and started giving me shit.

He had been wearing faded ski gear and his green eyes gleamed when I made a joke. It wasn't long before we were pointing at lines together off the chairlift, before we were sitting next to each other in the lodge bar drinking IPAs, before he was getting my phone number at the ski racks while the moon rose over the mountains. It wasn't long before the seemingly ordinary events of the day became solidified into part of the story we would tell later of how it all began.

Before we met, I had only backcountry skied in the east. I'd skinned up little hills on my street with my dad and done a skimo race at the resort and bootpacked up Tuckerman Ravine. He'd grown up on Colorado's Western Slope and had a master's degree in snow science, so I always relied on him to make the final call. If he thought it was safe, it probably was, and if he thought it wasn't safe, it probably wasn't.

***

He was the first person to look at me with tears in his eyes and whisper *you*. We sat in his kitchen with our legs intertwined and he told me he was in love with me, and all the reasons why.

He told me I was beautiful when my hair was a scraggly mess from being under a helmet all weekend and when I was in a big flannel on his couch and when I'd been in the backcountry for days and hadn't showered.

He held my hand when we walked down the street to the brewery in town and showed me all of his childhood places and took me on a river trip with all of his best friends. He called me his lady and talked about our future and missed me when I was gone. Late at night in a tent in Montana in the cold, with the rushing river lulling us to sleep, he held my face in his hands and told me I was what everyone was looking for and he had found me.

And I breathed out the breath I'd been holding my whole life, waiting for someone to make me feel this way. Waiting for someone to make me feel held and whole and worthy. He was there, so I was okay.

We're told the story over and over again. Love is something you must obtain from others. You are not whole until someone else arrives to make you feel worthy and valued, until someone else provides for you the things you need. We are told this story enough times that we think this is how it is, that this is how we are to live, that the story of our salvation will start with a lanky guy in a red Arc'teryx shell walking around a corner toward us in the parking lot.

***

In the backcountry you are only as safe as your weakest link. It's not like driving a car, where as long as the person at the wheel knows what they're doing, you're fine. As long as the person in control is experienced and knowledgeable, the person in the passenger's seat can nap or read or otherwise fail to pay attention to what is going on with the road. The backcountry isn't like that. There are no passengers, only drivers.

Terrain and snowpack assessment are crucial aspects of wintertime backcountry travel, and placing all of your trust in someone who is an expert is one of the six heuristic traps that often lead to accidents. It is referred to as the "expert halo," and occurs when a party lets one person drive the car and stops looking at the road. That expert may be falling into other heuristic traps (seeking social acceptance, not wanting to back down from an objective, feeling the need to get first tracks, allowing familiarity with the zone to affect their judgment), and, with no additional opinions from the group, these biases go unchecked.

To have a truly safe expedition, each member of the team must hold within themselves all the knowledge and experience necessary for success. They need to be able to assess the scene, to perform snow tests and analyze them, to form evidence-based opinions, to make informed decisions, to react in an emergency, to carry out a rescue. If each and every person in the party cannot do this independently, everyone is at risk.

We toured on Red Mountain Pass in the San Juans when I

was at his parents' house for Thanksgiving, and even though the extended column test we'd done had resulted in a score of 17/30, meaning that ten taps from the wrist and seven taps from the elbow had caused a propagating failure, we skied anyway. I didn't think to question it. I was relying on someone other than myself, placing the responsibility elsewhere, waiting for external confirmation. He was there, so I was okay.

***

There is a free avalanche awareness program out of Utah called Know Before You Go. It was started in 2004 as a way to educate youth about the dangers of avalanches and proper backcountry safety, and has since expanded to provide hour-long presentations to all sorts of interested parties. Know Before You Go encourages all those engaging in wintertime backcountry travel to have the proper information and education prior to embarking on any kind of mission or expedition. Its main aim is to reduce avalanche-related accidents, injuries and fatalities by urging backcountry enthusiasts to arm themselves with everything they need to be safe.

Before you wind up in a dangerous, high-stakes situation that could have been simply avoided, don't. Take an avalanche safety course, do beacon practice and read the avalanche report. Choose your terrain wisely and know your partners well and dig a pit. Know all this before you go.

What you don't know, the program says, can kill you. What you don't know can get you in too deep.

What I didn't know was a lot. What I didn't know was that all relationships are a reflection of your relationship with yourself. What I didn't know was that I, like all other human beings, was already a perfect, brilliant shard of the universe, enough just for existing. What I didn't know was that being alone is not worse than being with someone who gradually stops giving you what you need.

I didn't know before I went, and soon enough I would hear the proverbial *whoomph*, see the hairline crack spreading across the snow, feel the ground shift beneath me.

***

A persistent weak layer is a poorly bonded layer of snow caused by faceted crystals or surface hoar that gets buried by the next storm, pushed down and out of sight. But it lingers, lying in wait below the surface, until just enough force from above causes it to fail and the layer on top of it to slide. Persistent weak layers can form early in the season and lie dormant for months until they are suddenly, catastrophically triggered, often with feet and feet of snow on top of them ready to slide. What looks like a beautiful untracked face can become a path of destruction in seconds.

Based on the last storm or the latest conditions, a slope

may appear stable, but the weakness underneath persists un-detected, a ticking time bomb. It may be able to withstand a few easy turns at the beginning, but once you really lay into it, applying any kind of pressure, it'll go. Those first few turns were a dream, stolen moments from a reality that couldn't last.

At the beginning he looked at me and said *you*. At the beginning he told me he'd drag me with him wherever he went. At the beginning he leaned in.

At the end he was tired and wanted to sleep in his own bed. At the end he only ever said, "I love you too." At the end he walked out to his truck and told me he'd be thinking of me. He wasn't there, so I wasn't okay.

As his perception of reality, his version of events, his as-sessment of the terrain changed, so did mine. Because I was relying on him to provide it. And in the end I discovered I'd leaned all my weight on a weak layer that couldn't hold me. On a persistent weak layer that had been lying dormant in him all along. On something that in the end would fail.

What do you do then? What do you do when the person with all the knowledge makes a bad call? When you lose the driver?

You take a good hard look at yourself and you realize the way we've been shown how this works is all wrong. That if you are perpetually waiting for someone else to make you feel whole, you will always be putting yourself at risk. That only when you are truly self-sufficient will you be able to walk with confidence, knowing that whatever happens you'll be all right.

Because no matter what we tell ourselves, the risk of living in fear of being alone is far greater than the risk of being alone. The risk of never knowing your own worth is far greater than the risk of not having someone else to show it to you.

Don't wait for someone to tell you you're beautiful to know you're beautiful. Don't wait for someone to tell you they love you to be loved. Don't wait for someone to tell you you're worthy to feel worthy. Feel those things because you are those things.

Let people tell you you're beautiful and that they love you and that you're worthy. But let it be a confirmation of what you already know to be true. Let someone telling you the snow-pack is well bonded and stable on south-facing aspects be a verification of what you had assessed and determined your-self, not a conclusion you couldn't have reached alone. Let it be knowledge you carry internally, always.

**

A few months before he left, I finally took my AIARE Level 1 Avalanche safety course. He was not there to check my work or explain things to me or do it himself. It was me, with three other students, standing in a snow pit, forced to rely on our-selves. We spent two days doing stability tests and analyzing snowpack and doing beacon practice and planning routes and skiing. At the end of the weekend, I was handed a certificate that stood for the knowledge I now carried in my brain. For the knowledge that no one could take away from me, that I alone was responsible for.

I was now prepared to enter the backcountry entirely self-sufficiently. I didn't have to wait for someone to come along to make me feel safe. I could choose my partners based on who I wanted to ski with, not who I needed to get by. I could come to the table already equipped with everything I needed.

Being self-reliant isn't about not letting anyone else in. It's about letting someone into a house that's already been built, rather than hoping they show up with nails and a hammer. It's about the difference between need and want. The difference between seeking and being.

***

Months after he was gone, I skied into a backcountry hut with some friends. The sun glinted off the snow and poured in dusty spirals through pine boughs and caused us to roll up our sleeves. The mountains, giants of stillness, surrounded us on all sides, beckoning us up to the high country. Just before we reached the hut, we found ourselves at the top of a pass, in a world that was nothing but sky and rolling white on all sides. I breathed out a breath I'd been holding since he left.

I looked at the mountain faces across from us as we skied up, making observations about slide debris on certain aspects, weighing in on how we should travel across particular sections, pointing out patches of surface hoar as we passed it. I was a knowledgeable, competent, responsible member of the team. I was whole.

I was there, so I was okay.

WARMTH

We would always delay getting out of our sleeping bags as long as we could. We cooked breakfast in the vestibule of the tent, unzipping the inner door and sitting with our puffy coats on and our sleeping bags around our waists, trying to glean a little heat from the stove, or put ourselves in the path of the steam coming off the boiling water. I stayed in my sleeping bag to change out of my sleep clothes and into my hiking clothes, to deflate and roll up my sleeping pad, to pack my equipment into my backpack. We delayed, we hung there, clinging to the comfort until we could finally avoid it no longer – we had to leave the warmth and venture out into the morning and what awaited us there.

Being comfortable is stealthily dangerous, a silent killer. Being comfortable is nice; it's easy. Staying in your sleeping bag in the morning is nice, but it's never going to be more than that. It's never going to be dizzying or staggering or make your chest burn. It tops out at this perfectly lovely level of fine that gets stale after a little while.

It is often worse for things to be nice and easy than to be bad. When things are bad, there is motivation for change. There is an impetus for movement. You are likely to strive for something better, for something different. The unpleasantness of your circumstances makes this the obvious and only thing to do. But when things are nice and easy, that momentum is absent. There is nothing that is propelling forward motion. It is easy to be lulled into nice and easy, into comfortable, and to stay there well past the moment we need to leave. When things are bad, when we have to fight through to make things better, we at least gain the experience of struggle; we are at least strengthened by the process. We get nothing from being comfortable.

On October 26, 2012, we woke up at 3:30 in the morning on a glacier in New Zealand. The past 48 hours had been a grueling series of mental and physical trials that had left me drained and discouraged. Two nights before, we had stayed up through the night to brace our tent against 120 km/h winds that barreled down off the mountains and into the tunnel we were camped in. Every hour one of us would venture out into the frigid, unforgiving night and try to use one of the knots we'd learned to tie the snapped guy lines back together while we could still feel our fingers. The next day we'd had to hike several kilometers uphill onto the glacier, postholing through hip-deep slushy snow the entire way. When we finally arrived at the spot we'd planned to camp at, we had to spend the next four hours probing out a perimeter, building tent platforms and snow walls to protect our tents. By the time we ate dinner, it was 8 p.m. and all the light had drained from the sky, the peaks around us no longer casting their long, angular shadows on the snow.

We crawled into our sleeping bags immediately afterward, wasted of energy, huddling together to try to stay warm. It was at 3:30 after that night that we woke up, put on our crampons, headlamps, harnesses and avalanche transceivers, roped ourselves together in groups of four, and began to ascend Ashburton Glacier.

Others talked about it afterward as one of their favorite memories of our time in the Arrowsmiths. The stars glinting above our heads, the silence of the sprawling wilderness pounding in our ears, the crunch of the ice beneath our feet, the glow of the headlamps up ahead, our rope teams like tiny constellations in the snow.

It was one of my worst mornings. I was weak and lethargic and miserable. It didn't matter that we were on our way to summiting our first peak, that we were climbing on a glacier, that the peachy pink alpine glow was starting to hit the crests of the mountains above us as the sun prepared to emerge. I was sweating and freezing at the same time, my legs felt like crepe paper beneath me, and all I could think of was the warmth of my sleeping bag that I'd left behind. With each taxing, carefully placed footstep, I was longing for nice and easy.

Too often we allow ourselves to settle for comfortable because we are trying to avoid the struggle. We are trying to avoid the difficulty. We are trying to avoid moving uphill in the dark and cold. We think that, by not struggling, by not making ourselves get out of the warm sleeping bag, we are doing ourselves a favor. That we are avoiding suffering. That we are happy. We think nice and easy is something to aim for, something to aspire to. We allow ourselves to think being comfortable and avoiding unpleasantness is as good as it gets.

It is an indulgence, and the longer we allow it to go on, the more difficult it is to free ourselves from its grasp. The longer we remain in the cocoon of warmth, the less appealing leaving it becomes. The more complacent we become in the arms of nice and easy, the more sleepy and bewitched the simplicity makes us, the more we are selling ourselves short. The more we are settling. Nice and easy feels good, but it doesn't make us better.

Just before 7:30 a.m., we angled to the right to attempt the final pitch of our climb, our bid for the summit. Light had drenched our surroundings, the sun punching through a high-hanging layer of fleecy clouds in orange and gold. My rope team had been the first to leave camp hours before, and we were the first to climb, one by one, onto the snowy

knife-edge jutting 2236 meters into the sky. We carefully removed our packs, planted our trekking poles in the snow and
carved out seats for ourselves, watching the others gain the
final few meters of elevation to meet us. And though for the
entire morning I hadn't felt capable or energetic or enthusi-
astic, as I sat perched on the uppermost ridge of the glacier,
I was filled with an elation, a sense of accomplishment and
pride that seemed to overwrite all the struggling I'd done to
arrive here. I wouldn't have crawled back into that sleeping
bag for anything.

From our camp below, we could see the mountains directly
next to us, projecting directly up like saw-toothed walls. But
from the tip of 2236 I looked out at mountains as far as I could
see in every direction, ranges beyond ranges stacking themselves in never-ending, snow-capped tiers.

I have to remind myself in memory that the morning wasn't
just this unbelievable victory but actually a fairly dismal endeavor up until the final moments. But you forget that. You
forget that when you look back. It was a struggle, and that was
an important aspect of it, but you don't get the sunrise over
the mountains, you don't get the soaring ecstasy if you stay
comfortable in your sleeping bag with your eyes closed. You
have to get out in the cold, you have to climb uphill, you have
to work through your exhaustion and your bad attitude. You
have to push yourself. You can't stay still, and it's not fine or

easy. Not at the beginning or the middle or the end. You get the full range of the spectrum, from freezing and miserable to towering and triumphant. It's worse than fine and it's also better than fine. Stunningly, unimaginably, overwhelmingly better.

It would be simpler to settle for nice and easy, to stay in the sleeping bag. There is immediate gratification; there is warmth. There is no struggle, there is no discomfort, there is no discouragement. But there is also no triumph. There is no awe, no unbridled joy or boundless beauty. It doesn't push you; it doesn't make you better. It doesn't propel your life forward in ways you never imagined.

And even if life can't be that boundless and blinding and ignited all the time, even if you have to spend an overwhelming amount of time in the trudging-uphill-in-the-cold-and-dark part, once you know that kind of life exists, you will never be able to stop chasing it. A life that challenges you and astounds you and demands of you everything you've got and then a little bit more. A life that's sprawling and expansive and extraordinary.

Because there is a different kind of warmth, a kind that doesn't come from wrapping yourself in down or synthetic fill, a kind of warmth you create, that emanates from the deepest part of you, that stings and tingles and makes it a little hard to breathe. It's the radiance of the newly risen sun on your face, the burn of exertion in your muscles, the glow of the bright white light in the hollows of your chest. It's real and it's attainable. But you have to get out of the sleeping bag.

Flowing through the Footholds

The sun was beating down on my head and I couldn't move.

There was nothing wrong with my body, no injury or physical impediment to speak of, but I stayed still, feeling unable to pick up my legs or arms, unable to shift my weight. I didn't trust myself, didn't have confidence in my tenuous position hanging on to the slushy spring snow of the headwall. I was not in actual danger, at least not at that particular moment.

My feet were securely balanced on established footholds, my body weight was leaning into the snow, my hands shoved into the mush. I lifted one leg up, testing out what it would feel like to kick my boot up to the next foothold and shift my weight onto that leg, to push myself up a little higher, and immediately brought it back down, returning to my original position. It was too high up, the transition of weight too much of a stretch.

I looked up above me as my companions climbed higher and higher, the distance between us growing greater. I had no interest in looking down, back into the bowl below, where other skiers making the ascent behind me looked like pebbles in an immense snowfield.

I paused to take a few breaths, to calm my mind and think about what to do next. We had hiked up far enough that we were now on the headwall, a section where the climbing was so steep we had to abandon the use of our poles and move using our hands, knees and feet instead. Turning back at this point would be more dangerous than continuing forward – it wasn't an option. Trying to click into my skis on this grade would also be too risky. The only choice was to keep moving upward, up over the lip of the bowl and on to the gentler slope of the snowfield above. I knew this, logically, but I still couldn't move my boot up to the next foothold. The fear was visceral, and I felt pathetic. I was frozen.

A little over a year before I found myself clinging to the headwall of Tuckerman Ravine in the White Mountains in New Hampshire, I was lying on my stomach in a tent in Patagonia, listening to the rain beat down on the ceiling and reading by headlamp. I had downloaded *Flow: The Psychology of Optimal Experience* on my Kindle before leaving on my month-long trip through Argentina and was just getting around to reading it now that inclement weather had set in. For something that was fairly scientific and dry, the book had me strangely riveted. It was all about this concept of "optimal experience," a state of being author and University of Chicago psychology professor

Mihaly Csikszentmihalyi argues is the key to happiness. I instantly connected with what Csikszentmihalyi was talking about – a state of being where you are so focused on what you are doing that the world around you seems to fall away – an almost trance-like state where you are doing something purely for the sake of doing it. I thought of how I feel when I run, or hike, or write sometimes, or even when I get hyper-absorbed in a task as simple as peeling a clementine. Time falls away, you get lost in the rhythm of the task and external worries or stresses seem to grow quiet. Often even the sense of personal identity fades into the background – there is only the task before you. There is only movement.

Back on the headwall, I still wasn't moving at all. Gripping the grainy snow with my fingers and toes, I was absolutely concentrated on nothing but keeping myself anchored to the mountain, but I wasn't feeling particularly happy or fulfilled. The focus was certainly there, but what I was learning as the seconds ticked away and I still hadn't moved my boot from its foothold was that it's not just the focus alone that produces flow. There are two crucial factors that will only produce a flow state when both are present at high and complementary levels: challenge and skill.

What Ueli Steck, the late Swiss mountaineer, experienced when attempting first ascents in record times is flow, because a high level of skill was being brought to a challenging situation.

If either factor slides too far in either direction, the flow state is lost. Put Steck on a high school rock wall and the only state he'd be in would be a state of boredom. And on the headwall of Tuckerman Ravine, I was in a state of anxiety. What I had to do and what I felt capable of doing were disproportionate. The fact that I had only a month of mountaineering experience under my belt, that I wasn't equipped with crampons or an ice axe and that the steps had been kicked by people considerably taller than me were all factors equaling a deficiency on the skill side of the equation. So I wasn't flowing – I was freaking out.

I couldn't go back, I couldn't stay where I was – I had to move. But I needed to adjust the challenge to fit my skill. I needed to slide down the scale so the disparity wasn't so glaring. I couldn't change the grade of the slope, I couldn't conjure an ice axe and crampons out of thin air – but I could kick smaller steps. So I lifted my leg up again, and this time, instead of reaching for the foothold that was waist-high in the snow in front of me, I kicked a new one in at knee level and stepped up onto it. And, just like that, I was a little higher. I had moved forward. I focused back in on nothing but the soundness of my steps and the placement of my body weight. The bowl around me ceased to exist except for the square of snow I could see in front of me. And in that quiet, in that focus, I tapped into that ancient state that was all rhythm, all movement. My entire life, in that moment, was just placing each foot in the snow and shifting my weight up. That task filled all the spaces, expanded itself to become my entire present universe. I was lost in the flow, and before I knew it I had crested the lip of the headwall and arrived at the gently sloped snowfield above.

Csikszentmihalyi challenges the common assumption that we are most content in our times of leisure – that finding ourselves in a reclining chair on a sandy beach would be the pinnacle of human happiness. He outlines the important difference between pleasure and enjoyment, a distinction we often forget to consider. The key difference between pleasure and enjoyment is the amount of challenge that is involved. We get pleasure from lying in the sun, but we don't get enjoyment. Pleasure is lovely in the moment, but it's not a lasting happiness. Enjoyment comes from something that challenges us, from something that may not be at all pleasant in the moment but makes us more complex as a person for having experienced it – that pushes us beyond what we expected. Pleasure was cracking open a cold beer on the floor of the bowl after a day of skiing. Enjoyment was having climbed up the headwall and skied two difficult runs successfully.

The most important point Csikszentmihalyi drives home in *Flow* is that we can achieve the state through any activity, in any moment of our lives, as long as we cultivate the right mindset. You don't have to climb up a steep, snowy headwall to access it. In the thousands of interviews Csikszentmihalyi conducted, it was clear the happiest people were able to enter into a state of flow doing just about anything – even people who had what would appear to be mind-numbing assembly line jobs or who had extremely adverse life circumstances. The key was to constantly keep the level of challenge up, to continually improve one's skills. And the best part – we are completely in control of both of those things. We can either up the external challenge – find steeper, higher mountains to climb – or we can adjust the self-imposed challenge – go faster, kick better steps, move more gracefully. Or if we find ourselves in a situation whose challenge is above our skill level, we can adjust it by breaking it down into pieces, by taking smaller steps. By keeping the level of challenge appropriate to our skill level, we can steadily gain the confidence it requires to continue to push farther, reach higher. And by doing this, Csikszentmihalyi argues, we can achieve complex, genuine happiness, no matter where we are or what we're doing.

In the car on the way home from New Hampshire, I felt the warm, fuzzy tiredness you can only get after a day out in the cold. My muscles were sore, a sunburn had started to settle into my cheeks and I was in desperate need of a shower, but it all somehow equaled this smooth, deep contentment. We all kept saying what a great day it had been, a perfect day, and, despite my bout of terror on the headwall, I really, truly meant it. The challenge, the exertion and even the fear had brought about this golden afterglow, this feeling of having really *done* something. Of hitting a wall and pushing through it. Of getting to the top, coming back down and, despite everything, wanting to do it all over again. I felt the golden electricity emanate from the core of my being and flow through the rest of my body, fill the whole car and echo out into the mountains around us.

Leaving Room for Magic

When the bus rounded the corner and we caught our first glimpse of Bariloche, I was barreled by blue. The sky and the lake and the mountains and the trees – all of it seemed to come rushing at us past the window at a million miles an hour after a long overnight bus from Mendoza. The landscape had changed gradually, from the arid northern pampa to the saturated landscapes of the Lakes District. And now we were in Patagonia.

I was gripped by it, by everything before me – the three-dimensional reality of a place I'd dreamed about for so long. The old version, curated by guidebooks and imagination, receded into the background, instantly and firmly replaced by what was actually there. I pushed thoughts of logistics to the back of my mind and for a moment allowed it all to pass through me – arriving in a new place with nothing but a thorough exhilaration for getting to be where you are.

At the bus station in town, Marielle and I switched from a large double-decker overnighter to a smaller municipal bus we had been instructed to take. It was old and green and filled with local passengers and didn't have enough room for us. We crammed ourselves in, our enormous packs taking up the space of two additional people. The initial unadulterated joy that came with showing up somewhere new was always tempered by the anxiety of figuring out a new public transportation system, of finding your way.

We missed our bus stop by over a mile, and my whole body cringed as I was forced to yell "*Parada!*" at the top of my lungs and wiggle my way past dozens of disgruntled Argentines. We walked back down the busy road along the lake with no sidewalk, getting strange looks from cars and feeling the weight of our backpacks, experiencing distinctly the part of travel that isn't all blue lakes out bus windows. It would have been easier to navigate our way to a hostel in town, but instead, at the last minute, we'd opted to pass over all the sensible, prearranged lodging options, and so we found ourselves walking on the side of the road out of town, looking for a street not on our map.

We were couch surfing with Julian and Alex, two locals who had been recommended to us by another American we'd met traveling a few days before. Their house was at the top of a long dirt hill, which afforded it swoon-worthy views at a price for those on foot. Sweaty, exasperated and tense about what we were about to get ourselves into, we arrived at the little house on the top of the hill and knocked. But all that faded within minutes of entering. We spent the first evening talking and cooking food and being stunned by just how many people there are in every little corner of the world living their lives. I stared out at the sun falling behind the peaks and pine trees that night off their balcony and laughed in that way you do when things somehow just manage to work out.

The lengthy spreadsheet Marielle and I had created in preparation for our month-long journey from Northern Argentina down to Patagonia dictated a two-day stay in Bariloche, but from the moment we arrived, something inside me settled, wanting to slow our pace and stay awhile. The pines and the lake and the mountains harked back to summers of my youth spent in Maine, where, thousands of miles away, one was surrounded by the same elements. The flavors of the air were distant cousins who did not speak the same language but were nevertheless family.

Julian and Alex were two friends in their 20s, both climbers and snowboarders who worked at a hostel in town. Julian was short and gregarious, with kind brown eyes and a long black ponytail, and Alex waifish and quieter, with her hair dyed magenta. They were the kind of people who didn't just view travelers who came through as guests but as friends. We grocery shopped and cooked meals together, sat on the tile floor of their house and talked about life. Before we knew it, two days had turned into four, and we were still in Bariloche.

The final day found us licking giant cones of *dulce de leche* ice cream and petting Saint Bernards in the town *centro*, and by late afternoon we'd migrated to the beach with a giant thermos of *maté* and Julian's guitar. The mountains loomed quietly in stacks of blue across the lake, and the strains of songs we'd never heard filled the air. We ran down the pebbled beach and into the cold water, and it swirled all around us, the foreignness and magic of the entire trip, distilled into a single moment.

According to the spreadsheet, we should have already been gone.

These things happen if you let them, if you have the courage not to fill up all the spaces. It can be daunting, this void, this plan-less space, but there is also a humility to it. An acceptance that some things are unknowable until you get there, that the universe may, in fact, provide you with something you never could have dreamed up in a moment outside of this space and time. If your bag is packed full before you leave, there is no room to tuck in the treasures you find along the way.

The longer we traveled, the more space we started to leave. It was a bit of a thrill, getting off a bus in a town you'd never been to with no set place to stay and seeing where you would end up. A charming stray joined us for craft beer flights and a blazing sunset from our campsite in El Bolsón, we spent four nights backpacking through Parque Nacional Los Glaciares with a group of Americans we met on a bus to El Chaltén and, despite visa problems earlier in the trip, we crossed the border from Argentina into Chile without further comment.

The days of our journey dwindled down to single digits and we arrived in Puerto Natales, the town outside Torres del Paine National Park in Chilean Patagonia. We found ourselves walking toward town, with only a vague sense of where we were going and no preplanned accommodations booked for the night. Just outside the main square of town, on a street that sloped down toward the ocean, we found a backpacker's hostel run by Torres mountain guides and asked if we could pitch our tent in their backyard. For a grand total of $4 we had a spot to sleep, access to the cozy kitchen inside and enough stories to last us well into the night.

The next day we made our way up to the backcountry campground just below the namesake towers, prepared to stay the night and hike up to the viewpoint the next morning at sunrise. A creek ran through the wooded campground and there was a small A-frame hut near the trailhead that said "*guardaparque*" on it. It was hung with Chilean and Patagonian flags and bore a sign that instructed us to register with the ranger inside.

He was in his 20s, tall and lanky, with dark curly hair. He spoke to us in disjointed English until he realized I spoke Spanish. He told us his name was Sebastián and ushered us inside.

The A-frame was small, the first floor consisting of a sink

and a woodstove and some chairs and a bathroom, the two beds up a spindly ladder at the back of the room. Marielle and I sat on a bench and wrote down our names in the log, where we were from and how long we were staying. Sebastián told us then that we should come cook dinner on the woodstove with him later that evening since it was the off-season and the campground was almost empty. He and I kept looking at each other after he had gone quiet, and I noticed then that his eyes were wide and light brown.

The hut was already warm and smelled like smoke when we knocked on the door a few hours later. Sebastián made us *maté* and gave us bread he had baked himself in the woodstove. We sat in T-shirts and bare feet, talking about Chile and our trip and the wilderness, Spanish and English swirling around us in equal parts.

I told him that after this I'd be teaching English in Chile for a semester but had no specific plans beyond that. It was a massive, unaccounted-for space that confused family and friends trying to make small talk and occasionally left me paralyzed with fear. Sebastián grinned and took a sip of *maté*. The space didn't seem to confuse or concern him at all. For the first time, I felt like someone was looking at me like I was doing the right thing, like I had an empty plate in front of a vast buffet spread.

My favorite word is "*improvisar*," he told us. To improvise.

The night sky outside filled with stars, we drained the *maté* in our mugs, Marielle grew tired and, suddenly, inevitably, it was just him and me.

He poured us more hot water and I inched my wooden stool closer to his and time seemed to slow. He held my hands and asked me the story of each of my rings and I told him. He asked if I had any tattoos, and I extended my left foot, etched with the Spanish word *atrévete*.

In English, it clumsily translated to "dare yourself," a reflexive form of the verb not often used. I had gotten it to avoid living from a place of fear, to find the strength to grow wings on the way down. To create space to welcome in that which we cannot possibly anticipate. To leave room for magic.

Here, in Chile, I did not have to translate. Sebastián looked quickly back up at me with a wicked grin. "*Atrévete*," he said to me. *Atrévete*. And we both leaned in for the kiss we'd felt coming since he'd opened the door of the A-frame, the unpredictable, unintentional fruit that could have only been born of uncertainty.

People and decisions and time and circumstance will align themselves in the most astounding ways if you loosen your grip, if you allow things to form naturally, to flow into whatever reality they tend toward.

In this reality, in the backcountry of Torres del Paine, we fell asleep under thick wool blankets and southern hemisphere constellations glittering through the tiny window above us.

And when my alarm went off in the dark the next morning, he would ask me to miss the only bus back to the park entrance and I would find myself once again disregarding the plan.

When I left two days later, he would hand me a scrap of paper with his full name written on it, and I would watch the first rays of the sun turn the *torres* red, and then we would never see each other again, but for a moment we held each other and let it all be.

The room I'd left for magic shimmered with all it held, with all that could not have been predicted, reminding me how often we define space by its emptiness rather than its opportunity, its freedom.

When a Hard Left Is Right

"Uh, guys…"

We were at a trailhead parking lot two hours from the nearest paved road, with our gear exploded on the ground. Packs, clothes, food organized into labeled Ziploc bags, sleeping bags, tent, cooking gear, med kit, rain layers, bear canisters and five shoes. Five shoes.

Jess was looking at us like she didn't know whether to cry or throw something or curl up in a ball in the dirt.

We started searching frantically through the expansive pile of items, enough things for three people to live in the wilderness for two weeks. But we were unable to make the math add up. Three people, five shoes.

When it became increasingly clear that, despite the shoe having to be somewhere, it was, in fact, nowhere, we all stood and looked at each other.

Planning for this trip had started over a year before when Jules had suggested we hike part of the Colorado Trail. Over the course of phone calls and lunch-planning sessions when

I was home for Christmas, we came up with a plan: 150 miles from Gunnison to Durango over the course of two weeks. Jess jumped onto the plan at the last minute, making our duo a trio. Jules would be flying to Colorado from sea level the day before we were supposed to set out, I would be arriving the same day from leading a trip in Hawaii, and, in hindsight, the fact that the first 24 hours went the way they did was not a surprise at all.

Our best-laid plans to hit the road at 7:30 a.m. turned into us leaving closer to 10:00, and incorrectly entered GPS coordinates saw us drive in entirely the wrong direction. So, at 4:00 that afternoon, we were on the floor of my friend Colt's kitchen in Crested Butte sorting our food, four hours away from the southern terminus in Durango where we would drop one of our cars. We'd planned on dropping a car that morning and then continuing on to camp at our put-in point in the Gunnison National Forest before starting the trail in the morning. But after a flat tire scare on Red Mountain Pass, a steadily worsening cold and a lot of tense conversations about what had transpired, we rolled into Durango at 10 p.m. under a curtain of cold rain and knew we would be going no further that day.

What seemed like moments after we'd set up our tent, we were turning off our alarms and packing everything up again, setting off into the dark for a nearly six-hour drive to the trailhead. The last two hours of the drive were on bumpy dirt roads, with two full-on stream crossings in my Subaru hatchback.

And after a day and a half of gear shuffling, driving around half the state of Colorado and snapping at each other for wildly unreasonable things like wanting to stop for dinner before going to bed, we looked down at the ground and counted five shoes.

It was the kind of thing that made you want to lie on the ground with your hands over your face and just give up, or just sit on the tailgate and take pulls of the post-trail celebration whiskey at 11 a.m. It was the kind of thing that made you realize maybe if your trunk wasn't such a shit show you would actually be able to keep track of your shit.

We spent the first ten minutes talking in circles about the past, which is always a fantastic way to solve a problem. What idiotic, irreparable things have we already done that we have absolutely no power over now? Let's talk about those and drive ourselves insane. Maybe the shoe was on the living room floor in Crested Butte. Maybe it was in the other car. Maybe it was at the campsite in Durango.

After we'd indulged in finger-pointing our way down memory lane, we finally arrived at the only place in our lives where we have any agency: the present. The reality was we were two hours away from a paved road with six feet and five shoes, and all we could do was move forward from that truth, regardless of where the shoe was or whose fault it had been.

We began to discuss our options. Hike in Chacos until the next resupply point? Jess shook her head. Hard pass. Have Jess drive out and get new shoes and meet us somewhere further along the trail? Splitting up felt like the wrong play. Have all of us drive out to get Jess new shoes, skip the first few days of mileage and start at Lake City, where our first resupply point was?

The second the final idea hit the air, we all instantly exhaled, as if we had been waiting for it before the shoe had even disappeared. We all stood there for a minute, envisioning the possibilities. Not having to hike nine miles right now in our tired, half-sick condition, giving ourselves a little more flexibility on the back end of the trip, being equipped with the proper footwear, drinking beer and car camping that night at the trailhead. It quickly became obvious this was our path; that maybe losing the shoe was the precise catalyst we needed to take the advisable step back.

Before retracing our steps back out to the highway, we decided to attempt to organize our things so we were less likely to be parted with a necessary piece of gear going forward. We emptied out the car, yard-saled everything on the ground and packed ourselves back up neatly. Jules stopped in the middle of tidying up her double-trash-bag situation that was the rain-proofing strategy for her clothes.

"Uh, guys..."

We both looked over at Jules, who stood inside the passenger door with a look of disbelief on her face, holding a lone, formerly missing, shoe.

"You've gotta be kidding me."

We all looked at each other again, all feeling the same thing but not saying it. Did we have to go now? Now the reason for us changing the plan had been resolved? There was no reason for us not to just shoulder our packs and start hiking, and yet...and yet.

Sometimes we become so tied to a plan that we cannot see past, around or through it. We said we were going to do this, so that's what we're going to do. That's what we have to do. Often we forget to stop and ask ourselves if it's even what we want to do, if it's even what makes sense.

Ultimately, it all comes down to your objective. To the reason you're there; to what you're trying to accomplish at the end of the day. Depending on your objective, nearly any outcome can equal success.

We stared at the folded-up Excel spreadsheet I'd carefully crafted, detailing how many miles we'd travel each day, and where we'd camp, rounding out to an even 150 miles over 13 days. This was what we were supposed to do, and now we had no excuse not to do it.

But when we took a step back, when we zoomed out, it

became clear none of us wanted to start that day. All of us could do with a good night's sleep; a few more hours to hydrate and rest, and Jules needed a few more hours to acclimate. We could all use the extra time cushion on the back end to round up the cars and get back to Denver.

As we rehashed options again, now that the shoe was present, we realized it wasn't super important to any of us to bang out a specific amount of miles, to get from this exact spot on the trail to the southern terminus. What we were here to do was spend two weeks in the backcountry and explore the San Juans and immerse ourselves in beauty. And hacking off three days' worth of miles would interfere with none of those objectives. Altering the plan would not bar success.

So we shoved three people and six shoes back into the car, drove two hours back to the highway over the bumps and rocks and through the creek and found ourselves camped out that night on Spring Creek Pass, ready to begin with enthusiasm the next day. We sat overlooking the Gunnison National Forest drinking IPAs, and were glad we'd gone out of our way, that we'd lost the shoe, that we'd driven a Subaru with low clearance through a creek four times in a row. We were glad for all of it because it had brought us here, to a plan that matched our objectives, to a place from which we all felt ready to begin.

It's all about stepping back and asking some key questions. Where do you want to go? How are you going to get there?

What's your purpose? Answering the why will inevitably lead you to the how.

For the first five full days of the trip we were above treeline. On day 3 we slept at our highest camp, at over 12,800 feet. It had been a long challenging day filled with multiple pass ascents, a surprise pack of mountain llamas, an emergency afternoon bivy due to thunderstorms and debilitating altitude sickness for Jules and Jess. We'd run down a ridgeline in the rain and taken refuge in the tent for a few hours until the storm passed, eaten a quick dinner and begun to contemplate the task ahead of us for the next day.

Jess and Jules turned in early, while I remained on the little knoll above our tent, looking down into a massive drainage. Part of why I'd wanted to come out here on an extended trip like this was the freshness, the clarity, the focus that comes when you are in the wilderness for a while. I'd only experienced it before when out for at least a week – it took your body and mind about that long to really settle into the cadence of the wild. I wanted to revel in it, to soak it in while I had access to it, so each night I tried to take a while to myself to sit quietly and just look, just be.

After the first initial minutes of my body seeking the stimulation it was used to, everything inside me began to settle, to slow to match the pace of what was around me. I looked at the green snowy peaks stacked in rows pressing into the horizon, at the way the evening light played with the intermittent cloud cover, relics of a storm hours past. I studied all the tiny details of the landscape around me – the ridgelines, the valleys, the things I'd like to ski if it were winter. I thought about what it meant to be out here, days away from a trailhead, looking at this space that existed purely for its own purposes, a self-engineered universe we humans were lucky to get a glimpse at. And I was here, right now, at 7 p.m., with nothing in the world to do except bask in the glory. It was all a miracle. The longer I sat there, the longer I felt myself melting into it all, a piece of the wild making its way back home. Exactly what I'd come out here to do.

At four in the morning a week later, it was yet again time to change the plan. With water seeping through the tent floor and onto our sleeping pads, we packed up all our belongings and set off into the fog, ready to put down a 23-mile day and escape the incessant rain. Ten hours after that, we shoved our rancid gear into the trunk of Jess's car and took off toward town, every single bite of melted cheese telling us we'd done precisely the right thing.

We showered at the rec center and ate until we couldn't anymore and collapsed onto hotel beds and thought about how the trip hadn't followed the plan whatsoever and yet how we had gotten everything we wanted out of it.

We had hiked 130 miles over the course of 11 days. We had

basked in the sun and huddled through the rain. We had pushed through lung-busting climbs and hopped carefully through talus and stomped over snow and cruised along mellow single track. We'd slept in lush river valleys and consulted the topo in precipitous wildflower fields and eaten cheese sticks on sweeping ridgelines and plunged our bodies into freezing alpine lakes. We'd laughed, we'd suffered, we'd taken quiet time, we'd made decisions, we'd fallen into the natural rhythm of the sun. We'd dug catholes and patched gear and gotten lost and cried for a host of reasons. We'd felt defeated and triumphant, exasperated and elated. We'd wished it was over and we'd wished it would never end.

In the end, we'd gotten all we'd asked for. The full experience. The full range of life in the backcountry. And none of that was ascribed to a particular start date or trailhead or mile count. We had gotten where we wanted to go and been where we wanted to be, even though we'd walked away from the original plan.

There are many trails that lead to many places. And if you find yourself wanting to reach a different destination, it's okay to take a different fork – to make a hard turn, to take a left. Sometimes it's the only way to get where you actually want to go.

Don't walk blindly, assuming you must do what you had once planned. Look up. Your why will show you the way, if you let it.

Legends of the Fall

It was the time of year when it was hot in the city and cool in the mountains, when the clear skies and crisp air beckoned you to higher altitudes. The leaves were beginning to paint themselves in sleepy colors during their twilight days in preparation for the slow fluttering journey to their final resting place. The atmosphere was saturated with what was already gone and what was about to be, summer fading and winter still waiting. The hills gleamed gold as we wound up into them, the car's thermometer registering lower and lower with each rocky switchback. It was time to hunt down fall turns.

At the trailhead at the top of the pass, we swapped our Chacos for trail runners and strapped skis on our backpacks, setting off on the dry rocky trail toward our objective – Skyscraper Glacier, tucked just below the Continental Divide. Last year's snow clung in meager patches to the rock faces, and hikers seemed to wonder just where the hell we were planning on going.

It would be several hours of hiking before we would even

put our skis on, before we would come face to face with the permanent snowfield we'd chosen as our goal for the day. In the fall you have to want it, have to be willing to walk for it, have to firmly believe that, no matter what the circumstances, skiing is better than not skiing.

We followed the trail for a few miles, ascending from the top of the pass where we'd parked our car to the ridgeline. Off to our left in the valley we could see the bare runs of the nearby ski resort, still in a pre-season slumber. Here the bitter wind bucked us around, letting us know it wasn't July anymore. It felt right somehow, like coming home after a long journey, to be moving upward with skis on our backs.

We consulted the map and at the indicated spot we split from the trail, walking east toward the top of the glacier. Spreading out laterally, we each moved forward different ways in the same direction, no longer confined to a specific trail. We scouted entry points, reveling in the terrain assessment, risk management and critical thinking that make backcountry travel come alive.

From the peak, we picked our way down loose scree to the small bench at the top of the glacier and sat down to put on our ski boots. Finally out of the bitter wind that had whipped at us as we came over the Continental Divide to get here, we savored the sun beating down on us from above and the soft snow under our feet. We had reached what we'd set out to find, that magical white substance that gets us up before first light and summons us into the high country time and time again. Below us glittered two alpine lakes and a landscape entirely devoid of snow. Down there, it was autumn. But here, tucked high up in the alpine, lay a permanent pocket of fairy dust.

One by one we dropped in, traversing knee-high runnels and hop-turning through pockets of dirt and rocks until we reached a cleaner section down low that allowed us a few smooth glorious turns before the snow transitioned back into boulders. Before the glimmering illusion of winter vanished, as if it were a mirage.

Our joy echoed off the rock walls towering above us, the thrill of sliding quickly downhill on snow amplified by the fact that it was fall and we weren't supposed to be able to do this yet. After a zealous round of high fives, we sat down on giant boulders to take off our boots and wipe the mud off our skis. We cracked open some granola bars and let the we-just-skied-that feeling wash over us, lingering in the post-line glory for as long as we could. It wasn't a pow lap or an Alaskan spine or an elegant couloir, but it was September, dammit, and we had gone skiing.

On our hike back to the car, winding through subalpine meadows flecked with orange and yellow, we discussed whether this counted as the last day of the previous season or the first day of the next, getting technical about what season the snow had originated from. But we realized that perhaps we were looking at it all wrong – that skiing didn't belong to a particular season but to a particular frame of mind. That it would always be there for those who believed in it.

Reach

I remember the feeling in my stomach when the bus pulled out of the station and I turned to look at Portland, Maine, knowing it would be the last time it would feel like I lived there. It was the weighted version of bittersweet, this heaviness and lightness at the same time. Heaviness of what I was leaving behind, so real and palpable, and the lightness of what I was moving toward, nebulous and unknown. The moment of letting go had arrived.

It would be a year before I would even return to visit my home state. It would be a year in which my old life would give way to a different one, with new faces and kitchens and trail systems and drives home. And though I couldn't know it then, what that bus was taking me toward was bigger and grander and fuller than what it was driving me away from.

It is necessary to do this sometimes, to leave the concreteness of something good for the hopes of something great. Each time you do so, there is a storm of panic and dread and back-pedaling and wishing things could go back to a way they will never be again. But then there comes a sort of calm. Relief even. The moment of separation you feared has passed, and you now launch forward into the abyss, waiting for the new order to take shape. Waiting to land.

I had been stuck, in a way, though I was only vaguely aware of it. I was stuck in a life I loved, but that was too small, and would never fully satisfy me. It had become the worn and outgrown fleece you eventually have to give away because it's not keeping you warm anymore.

Thousands of miles away from Maine, I started bouldering at a gym in a warehouse near the Title I public elementary school where I taught fourth grade. Heights made me nervous and falling from them even more so – one of the reasons I made myself go once a week.

One day I stalled on a new route about halfway up the wall, secure in my current spot but hesitant to make the move to reach the next hold. Where I was, I was safe. Where I was, I wasn't going to fall off the wall. But I wasn't going to get up it either. To continue the climb, to push myself higher, I had to expose myself to that moment of instability, of uncertainty. I could stay where I was, clinging to the wall, safe but stuck, or I could reach toward what lay ahead.

I contemplated the move for longer than my muscles wanted to cling on to the wall, considering how I could twist my hips or rearrange my footing to best position myself to get my left hand up to a hold high up above my reach. Each time I reached the moment of truth, I froze, clutching my comfortable position.

The safeness you feel is a trap – it's keeping you in place when you must push off from your holds and withstand the uncertainty of whether you will meet your objective or fall flat on your back. There will always be that moment where you don't know, where you aren't sure about anything and where it feels like maybe letting go of what you are sure of would be the craziest, stupidest thing you could ever do.

I knew my arms had a finite amount of strength in them, and I could use that strength to cling in place, or I could use it to climb. So I hurled myself up toward the next hold, stretching out my fingers and grasping hard. And, suddenly, I was there. The panic and dread and backpedaling were gone and I was on the other side.

You must try to live a life that is expansive, that spreads you into the tiniest corners of yourself, that fills you to the brim. If you are feeling small, it's time to go.

The things I left behind in Maine would always be a part of me. They would always mean something. You cannot reach the top of the wall without putting your fingers and toes on all the holds at the beginning and in the middle. But leaving meant something too.

A house tucked into the foothills would replace my

childhood room in my parents' home. An MA would join my BA. A cubicle and a headset would become the faces and minds and hearts of 24 tiny humans. Small love would give way to big love. Rounded, tree-covered mountains would fade into jagged, snow-capped peaks.

You must not settle for halfway up the wall. You must reach. Even if that reach involves you springing bravely off your solid footholds and hoping like hell your arms can get you where you need to be. Don't wait too long. Don't overthink it. Go.

The Things We Carry

There are a million ways to try to hold on to things. We close our eyes, we narrate, we imagine, we recreate, we pinch our fingers, we clench our fists, we stare and stare and stare. We clutch and we grab and we cling, trying to keep what has already passed. We seem to be programmed to resist the shift, resist the transformation of things ending. To ease the ache, we often try to create physical artifacts of what has slipped away, of what we have left behind us.

Photographs turn memory into public property, turn moments into something stiff and unnaturally glossy. When there is a photographic representation of a moment, it suddenly becomes the signifier, the primary representation of that moment. Perhaps as time goes on we begin to remember the photograph instead of the moment itself. Those moments you can hold in your flattened palm. What you have to hold differently are the moments that live only inside your head, the ones the camera didn't catch, the ones you maybe can't see, but you can feel. Those require cradling, require cupped fingers.

In New Zealand we took pictures at the top of peaks when the sun was out, we took pictures when we turned a corner and were stalled by the expanse of scenery before us. Those moments, too, are memories. Those moments were beautiful and important. But the moments I'll cradle, the moments I'll cup my sunburned fingers around, are different ones. The ones I can feel more strongly than I can see.

All of us standing in the driving rain at the top of a leafy ridge, thoroughly soaked through our neoprene, looking out at the ocean, waiting for a window to make the final paddles of a journey. The way the light came through the yellow tent ceiling as we sang Ingrid Michaelson's "You And I" after I ran through the thick silent snow to get there, realizing I had remembered the words. The inexplicable warm calm that came over me as I sat up in the middle of the tent through the night, bracing it against roaring winds funneling themselves in over craggy mountaintops. The hugeness of the silence the morning we climbed up a ridge guided by headlamps to watch the sun emerge.

The freezing electric jolt to our entire energy when we flung ourselves into an alpine lake still cased with ice. The tumbling inertia of laughter it took only a look to set off. The feeling of fleeting togetherness as we sat on top of box containers watching the sun go down for the last time, the strains of the guitar Colt held in his hands filling the atmosphere. These were the things that lived only inside us, that we would have to hold closer to keep, or perhaps hold in a different way.

The last day out in the field we moved slowly. We took longer to pick up our feet, we chose routes that led us out of the way, we stood contemplating more deeply where to cross a river. We took breaks even though we weren't tired, we baked a pie on the side of a hill in our sleeping bags, we spent hours huddled against our backpacks, hiding from the wind, watching the rising sun burn the bottoms of the clouds red. We did all these things and yet we still came to the finish, we still popped up over the last hill and saw the way out, the way to the end.

No matter what measures we took to prolong it, the end continued to loom, waiting for us to arrive. We stopped on a wide flat hilltop and shrugged off our packs, quiet. Justine suggested we do cardinal acknowledgements, a sort of Maori yoga practice we had learned that brings you closer to the earth – acknowledging north, south, east and west, sky, self and earth – that allows you to push out all the curling black smoke within you and gather in all the incandescent white light of your surroundings.

The five of us stood in a line, spread out across the hilltop, and repeated the motions facing north, south, east and west. We opened our arms up to the sky, brought them down close to our chests, bent low and grazed the grass with our fingertips. We pushed out the fear and the sadness and the negativity, we pulled in the power of the mountains, the freshness of the air, the warmth of the sun, the calm of the sky.

We faced each direction and said thank you, and at the end we turned in toward each other and said *namaste*, the light in me acknowledges the light in you. We all stared down at the patch of beech trees winding through the valley toward the road beyond it, knowing there was a sort of bittersweet inexorability bringing us toward it. Each step we took contained the thousands of other steps we had taken over the previous months – sidesteps across swift and murky rivers, lunging leaps from one boulder to the next, plunging postholes deep into mushy snow, careful footfalls along narrow footpaths, triumphant strides up the last few meters of elevation gain.

These steps were the same as thousands of others, and yet they were different because they were the last ones. Because when we set our packs down, it would be for the last time. When we pulled our boots and gaiters off and laid our socks out to dry, it would be for the last time. When we did everything we had been doing for months, it would be for the last time. The magic, the spell of perpetual skin-tingling awe that had wrapped itself around the entire expedition, would be broken. But no matter how languid we allowed our cadence to become, no matter how many times we paused, the only direction in which we could move was forward.

John Muir wrote, "These beautiful days must enrich all my

life. They do not exist as mere pictures – maps hung upon the walls of memory – but they saturate themselves into every part of my body and live always."

The way we hold on to things isn't through two-dimensional snapshots or even written words. It isn't through retelling, through mentally recreating, through nostalgic daydreaming. Even when we must walk away, we can hold on by reaching out our arms and gathering it all into our chests, by carrying the muscle memory of all our footfalls with us as we take our next steps. By letting the sun seep into our skin, by letting the mountains press themselves up against us, by letting the air fill our chests, by keeping the electricity buzzing through our veins.

The way to truly hold on to things is not to attempt to preserve memories that immediately begin to fade and curl at the edges but to allow the experience to inform every step we take afterward, to evoke the spirit, the energy, the essence of it all in everything we do. The actual expedition may have been over, but it would be palpable in everything we did next.

One of the principles we were taught in our Leave No Trace training was "Leave what you find." But we hadn't. We couldn't. Every incline we had panted up, every shoreline we had washed our dishes at, every scree field we had sidehilled, every sunrise we'd snuck out of the tent early to watch, every patch of matagouri we'd hurled ourselves through, every gust of wind we'd stayed up bracing the tent against, was now an indelible part of us, glowing through our rib cages and out the tips of our fingers. We couldn't have left what we'd found if we'd wanted to. And while we stretched out our arms on the hillside at the end and tried to hold on to everything that had happened, it became clear it would also be holding on to us.

OR

I woke up at 10 p.m. and lugged my gear out to the start line. Pack, helmet, skis, poles, boots, avalanche safety equipment, 4,000 calories worth of snacks, 8.8 pounds of water and two flower hair elastics wrapped around my braids. The base of Mt. Crested Butte was dotted with hundreds of headlamps, and the air stirred with pent-up energy about to be released. I clicked into my bindings, took a few deep breaths and steadied myself. I thought the hardest thing I was about to do was ski 40 miles through the dark to Aspen.

My race partner Lindsay and I were skiing in the Grand Traverse, a backcountry ski race between Crested Butte and Aspen that attracts hundreds of hopefuls a year and churns out only a fraction of finishers. Months of preparation had brought us here, to 11:59 p.m., the moment we started striding into the great blackness.

A collective inhale, a gunshot, and it was happening. The crowd surged forward, hundreds of hearts beating uphill, and within minutes began to diffuse, settling into their positions, falling into the steady rhythm of ski touring. The beginning of the race would find us crossing creeks, sidehilling drainages and hauling ourselves up steep bootpacks, with nothing but the headlamps of those before us as a guide.

The night is such a massive numbing thing. Hours passed without delineation, every step up a gradual, treed drainage feeling exactly the same as the thousands before it. The night turned the mountain landscape around us into nothing, into a vast emptiness that offered us no landmarks, no milestones. The time on our watches felt arbitrary; simply a reminder of when to eat a snack.

We suddenly found ourselves at miles 9, 13, 16. Daylight keeps clearer watch over what we have accomplished and what we have yet to attain, and the night lets it all slip into an ill-defined dreamscape.

But in the darkness we also felt strong. When you couldn't see anything, you couldn't see how far you had to go, couldn't measure yourself up against a sprawling distance ready to swallow you whole. The tiny orb of light around the tips of our skis cast by our headlamps became our entire universe. We knew how far we would have to go, but, as far as we could see, all we had to do was take one more step forward.

We arrived at the first checkpoint at 6:11 a.m., nearly an hour ahead of schedule, ready to gulp down our allotted eight ounces of boiled snow and prepare for the climb up Star Pass.

We had been on track to make it between 5:00 and 5:30 a.m., but we had slowed in the final miles leading up to the hut. We were both tired and hungry and ready for the sun to be up. I was rejuvenated at the sight of a concrete indicator of our position on course, and felt confident we would make it to Aspen. But we had already begun on a trajectory that would take us on a different journey from the one we anticipated.

To get here, we'd trained for months. Long hours on flat slogs where we didn't rip skins, crazy weeknight missions comprised of more driving than skiing, endless discussions about gear tinkering and food strategy. We'd both trained through illness and weathered blisters larger than any coin in circulation, both dumped money into moving faster with less weight, both spent hours inside our own heads wondering if we were strong enough to do what we had signed up to do.

The months had turned into weeks, the weeks into days, and suddenly we found ourselves wandering around Crested Butte, staring down the barrel of the start with only a few hours to go. All of the minutes spent training and preparing and steeling ourselves came down to this – whether or not we could actually strap skis to our feet and make it across the Elk Mountains to the finish.

Even though I had never been to the sundeck at Aspen Mountain, I had envisioned myself arriving there hundreds of times. Sweaty, tired and overflowing with gladness and relief, crying tears of joy as I transitioned my skis from uphill mode to downhill, preparing for the sweet three-mile descent to the finish. I teared up several times just thinking about this moment, able to feel so viscerally that singular chest sting that comes when you have accomplished something you always knew you could and weren't sure you ever would. I played it over and over again in my head, a carrot to get me through long workouts that sometimes felt like pointless self-imposed misery.

I was in it for the chest sting. I was in it for the happy tears. And that meant I was in it for all of the suffering that came first.

Around 4:30 a.m., Lindsay had started having to pull over more frequently to catch her breath and take her inhaler. I remembered our first meeting after we decided to do the Grand Traverse together, in a brewery after a day of resort skiing. We'd devoured burgers and scribbled down notes to organize the enormous multi-pronged task that lay ahead of us. She'd mentioned she had exercise-induced asthma but didn't seem concerned about it. We trained for nearly six months, and it hadn't been a significant interference. She was strong and meticulous and determined, and she'd be able to breathe easier when the sun came up.

We had an hour and 49 minutes to make it up and over Star Pass. The angle of the incline increased sharply and I skied behind Lindsay, using the post-checkpoint resurgence of energy to shout encouragement as she continued to move slowly. I started picking landmarks a few yards away that we would make it to in order to chunk up the climb. We'll ski to that flag. We'll ski to that switchback. All we had to do was make it up over this pass, and then we'd get to descend. She just needed to get to the bonfire aid station after the descent, she said. There we'd eat and drink water and rest and she'd be fine to make it to Aspen.

After ten minutes, I told another pair passing us that we needed their towrope. We hadn't brought our own. All throughout our training, including the 23-mile training race we'd done in Crested Butte a month before, the idea of having to tow another person at any point seemed ludicrous. But now it seemed it would be the only way we'd make it in time. The blazing alpenglow was starting to creep down the peaks behind us at a rate faster than we were moving. We were losing our window.

I attached the rope to my pack and to Lindsay's hip belt and began towing her up the pass. Our pace dipped more and more as we continued, stopping more frequently and for longer stretches. I towed her through the bootpack and up onto the top of the ridge, where she put skis back on and I continued walking, pulling her behind me. Our generous lead was dwindling to mere minutes. The checkpoint was in sight, the sun threatening to vanquish the ridge.

As the stops became more frequent, the balloon in my chest that had inflated at the sight of the gathered headlamps marking the Friends Hut checkpoint began to crease and wrinkle. After months of wondering if I would be strong enough, fast enough, I was here, past the checkpoint, feeling ready to tackle the nearly 25 miles that still lay ahead of us. My eyes were clear, my legs were strong, my lungs were firing on all cylinders.

And yet, as I inched across the ridgeline, I began to know something I didn't want to know yet. I watched as team after team passed us and the time window shrank, and I began to know I was strong enough to make it to Aspen, but that didn't mean I would.

I turned around to Lindsay, the words catching on their way out, stinging my eyes. "Even if this is it – I'm glad we're out here."

It would have been easier to be angry. It would have been easier to grow quiet. It would have been easier to sink into bitterness. It also would have been easier to not try to ski 40 miles, but here I was.

Somehow, even in that knowing, even in the acknowledgement of an outcome I didn't want to face – a perfect opportunity to show up as someone other than my best self – I felt drawn out, drawn up – I heard the whisper of *or*.

Or you could rise. Or you could take care of your partner in the way you'd want her to take care of you. Or you could pay attention to how magnificent the sun on that ridge looks. Or you could choose light and love, regardless of the circumstances. That *or* is always available to us, no matter how vehemently we pretend it's not.

I let my eyes sting for a brief moment, allowing the frustration that comes when reality fails to meet our invented expectations. It is one of the most futile emotions we entertain – mourning something that never existed as if it had been promised to us.

I had signed up to ski from Crested Butte to Aspen because it was a challenge and an adventure. And none of the things that were occurring now, not the asthma or the lost time, were interfering with either of those goals. We were still out here. We were still challenged. We were still having an adventure. So I did what I had within my power to do. I made the choice that is always there, waiting. I chose to rise. I kept moving forward, and I embraced the Or.

We made it to the Star Pass cutoff by six minutes, hustling across the line to transition to downhill mode for a sunny, variable descent into another basin.

By then the sweepers had caught up to us, confirming our recent acquisition of last place. The bonfire aid station was being dismantled and the racers resting there told to get a move on.

"What are our options?" I asked the sweepers, out of her earshot.

"Five miles up to Taylor Pass where they can get a sled in. Or 18 and a half back to Crested Butte."

Forward. The only direction we could go was forward.

We began sidehilling through a thick forest, the sun spiraling through the trees in a way that was too beautiful to ignore, even under the circumstances. How could I be mad? What was the point of resisting what was? We were still out here. We were still traveling through a staggering backcountry basin. We had still skied over 20 miles.

I kept towing Lindsay, feeling the strength in my legs that could have taken me to Aspen still spring-loaded. It became increasingly clear her condition would not improve on its own, that we would not make it together. She had ripped skins and clicked into her bindings, and I was pulling her at a dead tow to decrease the amount of exertion required on her part, and we were still hardly moving. The albuterol was not helping her breathe. The only thing to do was to get her out.

I felt the determination to make it to Aspen release from inside me, floating up into the snow-covered pines. The energy, the focus and the persistence would still be required, but I would need to channel them in a different direction. We were deep in the backcountry, her asthma attack was escalating from mild to severe and I was the most medically qualified person around with a Wilderness First Responder certification. I looked at her sitting on the snow on the side of the trail, white-faced and blue-lipped, staring at her feet and wheezing audibly, and knew my mission had shifted.

I saw the two paths laid out before me, like skin tracks through the snow. I could resent her, resent the situation, resent the months of training that would now be for naught. I could feel frustrated that my opportunity to finish the race was being taken from me. Or I could accept what was happening as the only reality I had to contend with. I could step into the first responder role with love and compassion and kindness. I could see this experience for all of its richness and opportunity rather than its disappointment.

The choice before me was the choice that is always before us. Would I be the best version of myself or another one?

As the midday sun beat down on us in a wide-open basin, we finally arrived at a place where the safety crew could get a snowmobile in. Without much discussion of a plan, except that she would be taken to Aspen and put on oxygen, Lindsay grabbed onto a rope and was towed away by the snowmobile. After struggling through the last 11 hours together, I found myself suddenly, unceremoniously alone.

In the next six hours, I would ski up to the top of Taylor Pass and then be told I couldn't finish without a partner. I would clutch a snowmobile I had been told was taking me to Aspen and be dropped off at the Barnard Hut aid station five miles down the trail. I would sit at the aid station and drink soup and put on my puffy and think my day was done. I would shrug my shoulders and get back up when officials asked if I was okay to ski the remaining ten miles of the race, and I would go.

Late in the afternoon, when nearly all of the racers had been in Aspen drinking beer and wearing sandals for hours, I would drag myself up Richmond Ridge in the company of a stranger, someone else whose partner had been evacuated. The slushy snow would glop up on my kicker skins, the sun would beat down unrelentingly through the trees, and I would continue.

All told, I would ski over 30 miles and spend 17 hours in ski boots. I would feel it all. The soaring moments in the burgeoning daylight arriving at Friends Hut, the bittersweet acknowledgment of unexpected challenge, the clarity and focus while handling an emergency situation, the reluctant acceptance of my race being over and the slow resignation of beginning again.

When I reached the sundeck on top of Aspen Mountain at 4 p.m., I did not cry. The moment was nothing like I had imagined. I didn't feel the chest sting, I didn't experience the happy tears. I was alone, exhausted and worried about a partner I hadn't seen in hours. I didn't revel in the moment, I didn't soak it all in, I just transitioned to downhill mode and pointed my skis toward the finish. I felt that specific way you feel when you've gone through an intense experience: slightly in shock, kind of amazed and fully aware that no matter how many times you tell the story, no one else will be able to fully understand what you've gone through.

After two hours on oxygen in an ambulance, Lindsay was rattled but fine, waiting at the base lodge for me after hours of having no idea where I was. In the coming weeks, we would spend long car rides and hot spring soaks and ski parking lot tailgates debriefing it all, but for now it was just over.

I was in this strange in-between state. I hadn't done the race, but I hadn't *not* done it either. I had skied over three-quarters of the course, towing my partner for five of the steepest miles, and been out for far more hours than most of the racers – nearly three times as long as the winners. I had done less, and also more.

Sometimes we believe we are preparing ourselves for one challenge, and it turns out we are being handed another. I had trained for hours in the snow and spent hundreds of dollars on gear and talked strategy into the ground. I had mentally prepared myself to suffer, and to continue to suffer. I had even floated the possibility that we would not ski fast enough to make the cutoffs; that we would be turned around at Friends Hut or Star Pass.

But what actually presented itself was something entirely different. A twist. A soft tap on the shoulder. A challenge that would have less to do with training and hydration and quick transitions and calories consumed, and more to do with empathy and acceptance and love.

The chest sting would come, but not until later, driving to work, when I suddenly came to understand what it all meant. When I suddenly came to understand that the experience I had been given was not an endurance race but a chance to show up as the best version of myself. I hadn't skied 40 miles, but I had done that. I thought of the moment on top of Star Pass when I embraced the experience I was actually having versus the one I thought I should have, and how that, more than anything else, was what it was all for.

It's that moment of *aw, shit*. That moment of knowing the universe is serving up exactly what you need and it's not what you thought you were getting. It's looking that *or* in the face and taking it by the hand.

It's choosing to rise.

Triangulation

If you are lost in the backcountry and unable to locate your exact bearings, you can use a technique called triangulation to find your way again. Triangulation involves a map, a compass and an identifiable feature – a point of reference you can see in order to determine your position. To figure out where exactly it is you are, and how to get back to where you need to be. Tall mountains, visible above fog or inclement weather, are a good place to start.

This happens – we round a corner and find ourselves somewhere we never thought we'd be, somewhere we didn't know we were. We realize we have strayed the course. And to find our way back to where we need to be, we need a point of reference to guide us. Something to stand tall and strong and visible against the fog that led us wayward in the first place.

One warm night in early spring, the person I loved walked into my house with an unfamiliar look on his face, and a few hours later walked out of my life forever. In the moments after he left, I looked around and realized I had no idea where I was.

It was a dizzying place in which so many of us have found ourselves: without the person we thought would stay.

How had I gotten here? How had I ignored all of the signs that I was making a wrong turn leading up to this? In my desire to follow this person, I had lost sight of the path. I had lost my bearings.

I didn't know how I'd gotten here, and yet here I was. And from here, I had to begin. From here, I had to walk myself back to my own personal path of righteousness. The path of my best life. I would have to use reliable points of reference – things I knew to be true and real – to point my feet in the right direction.

* * *

Four years before, I woke up in the middle of the night in New Zealand. I was sleeping outside, and had been awoken by the cold air on my nose, or perhaps the universe. I had spent the previous few days in a panic about where my life would go after I left the wilderness. About where I would be and who I would be with and what I would do. About all of the things that ground us.

But when I awoke that night, the stillness of the vast landscape around me seemed to quiet the whirring panic in my brain. I didn't know necessarily where I would go, or whom I would be with, or what I would do. But I knew in that moment how I would need to feel, to be true to the truest part of myself. I would need to constantly present myself with challenges to grow and evolve. I would need to surround myself with people who brought out and celebrated all the intricacies of my heart and mind and soul. I would need to be in places that made me cry out at the beauty of the earth and allowed me to explore it. I would need to live in a big, sprawling, limitless way. Learning and giving and reaching and dancing.

I knew the path wouldn't be flat. I knew it wouldn't always be well marked. I knew there would likely be bushwhacking involved. But I knew it would lead to the clearest alpine lakes, the brightest wildflowers, the craggiest peaks and the most golden sunrises and sunsets. It would lead to the purest feeling of joy in my soul, when I was viscerally aware of and wildly grateful for my presence as a human on this planet. I looked up at the black silhouettes of the peaks around me, the southern hemisphere constellations gleaming brilliantly above my head, and I knew I must live my life boldly chasing this feeling or I would never be truly happy.

We have no way of knowing what our lives will bring us – what events will transpire or people we will bump into, where we will go or what choices we will make. But we can identify that satisfying, soul-level *click* that occurs when everything is just right, when we are where we're supposed to be at the moment we're supposed to be there. When the environment is just right for us to be our best selves, and when the people we are with reflect that best self back to us. We can identify that feeling as the true reason we are here and do whatever it takes to set our lives on that course.

I have always imagined a future version of myself out up ahead, looking over her shoulder, holding out her hand to beckon me forward. *We're just up here, just a little farther now, and it's glorious.* I envision the future version of myself that has transcended a difficult moment, that has figured out a tricky situation, that has the answer to a burning question. I imagine her out there waiting for me, and it's a sort of comfort. Future me has gotten through this. Future me is winking and twirling and laughing in slow motion and holding out her hand and whispering *just you wait.*

* * *

I wasn't completely lost, merely sidetracked. Merely in a situation that required a little triangulation. I had found myself alone and responsible for navigating myself through the fog. So I reached down into the depths, and I conjured up that night in the New Zealand backcountry, trying to locate those black silhouetted peaks and southern hemisphere constellations. With them as guides, I could plot my location on a map, and I could determine the course I would be required to take to return to the path of my best life. I would have to walk myself back through any number of obstacles, but I could get there from here.

You need to maintain that faith, that even when putting one foot in front of another seems like the most taxing exercise imaginable, that you must do it, and you will. That even taking tiny slow steps out of the woods will get you back to the path. That your best life is out there waiting for you. Eventually, you will be where you need to be. You're already on your way there.

Sometimes I'd arrive at that place up in the distance and realize *I* was the future me I had been looking at. That I was the one winking and twirling and imagining myself six months before thinking *if you only knew*. I would realize I had made it, and I would smile and wrinkle my nose and laugh in that way you do when life is strange and wonderful and unbelievable all at once.

From here, from this journey out of the woods and back onto the path of my best life, I look up ahead through the fog and I see the twinkly-eyed girl who looks like me, only calmer and wiser. She turns back toward me as always, reaching out her hand. On her right shoulder are the black silhouettes of peaks and a southern hemisphere constellation, my points of reference through the fog, calling me forward onto the path and into the light.

In the Thick of It

We had been hiking for seven hours in the Tetons and I was done. I'd left my trail runners in a friend's car and each step in my clunky old hiking boots tore at the back of my heels. We'd hiked out of our backcountry campsite at Surprise Lake from the night before, gotten in the car, driven to the Paintbrush Canyon trailhead and begun hiking again, wading with our giant backpacks through day hikers in jeans at Leigh Lake to get into the woods. The scenery changed every couple of miles as we ascended, thick forest shifting to boulder fields and finally opening up into a wide bowl flecked with patches of stale snow still clinging on.

Sometimes hiking you feel strong, energized by your muscles working to get you where you want to go, revitalized by the fresh air and scenery around you, and other times you feel like you want to find the nearest flat spot of ground and curl up and sleep. So much of it is in your head, so much of how you feel and how you experience the time passing can be linked to the thoughts passing through your brain, and today I was tired, I was fed up and I was ready to be done. My feet hurt, my legs ached and my pack felt like it was crushing me little by little. I was in one of the most beautiful places in the country, but destination desire had set in and all I wanted to be doing was sitting in camp, eating dinner straight out the pot.

These moments happen often, moments where the one thing that feels most difficult to do, to go on, to keep moving, is the only thing we can do. Moments when our feet hurt and the load on our back is heavy and our attitudes suck and we are still miles from our destination. It's easy to let the negativity build, to enter a mental state of misery and defeat. All we can see is how far away the destination is and how many steps we have left to take.

We were nearing the back of the bowl when my cousin Julie and I started to make stupid, naive comments to each other about how high the walls were and wondered where the trail was going to go next. Our campsite for the next evening was in the canyon over, so there had to be a notch somewhere, right? A col? Anything that was lower than the towering rock walls looming above us. But as we continued to ascend through slushy snowfields, it soon became clear the only way this could go was up and over.

I saw it first, the switchback that cut across the steep narrow scree field in between two peaks. I laughed and Julie looked up. I just pointed at it, at where we would have to go, and we both stopped. The run out was thousands of feet of loose scree peppered with stretches of thin snow. After the first switch-back, the trail seemed to disappear, with only this faint idea that somehow we were supposed to end up on the ridge above.

We briefly reviewed self-arresting technique and set off across the snowfield toward our imminent ascent, knowing the day was waning and we still had to get up, over and down into the canyon next door, ideally before nightfall. The switch-back, though appearing well defined from a distance, turned out to be less wide, less stable and less clear than we'd antici-pated. Training my eyes to focus on the ground ahead and not the drop-off below, I began to make my way across, checking in with Julie every few steps to make sure everything was still a go.

Something happens when you enter technical terrain, when things become difficult in a way that requires not only stam-ina but intense focus. No longer are you able to think about the entirety of the distance in front of you, of how long you have before you can rest – all of your mental energy is required for each step. The scope gets smaller, the lens narrower, until nothing exists in the universe except finding a stable place to step.

Across the switchback we reached the base of the far peak and the trail disintegrated. With the peak to our right and a steeply angled snowfield to our left, the option to sidehill disappeared, and the only way to go was straight up the scree. We took turns scrambling up, shouting directions to each other and staying out of the fall line. What had before been a weary fatigue in my legs had turned into a nervous weakness. Each time the scree slid from out below my feet my entire body tensed, sensing if not seeing the long fall that would await if I were to lose my footing.

After we slowly but safely navigated ourselves up to slightly more solid ground, the trail vanished entirely. I started to scout a route up to the left that I didn't feel great about, but it seemed to be one of our only options. As I started to move up the rock, a voice called out from what seemed to be the heavens. "The trail is up to the right!" it said. I swiveled my head around, disoriented, wondering if the mountain gods had finally decided to intervene so we wouldn't end up killing ourselves on terrain we hadn't been prepared for. Instead, I saw two tiny figures standing up on the ridge above us, pointing at the right side of the chute. From where we stood, it was impossible to see where the trail went – we were too close to it. But from their perch up on the ridge, our two hiker angels had a perspective we didn't – one that allowed them to see the exact route that would take us where we wanted to go.

Once I had backtracked and met Julie at the top of the scree slide, we located the faint trail and followed it up toward the crest of the ridge. We were so close, only a few dozen steps

separated us from the top of the ridge. Julie, a climber, negoti-
ated herself easily across the cruxiest spot of the whole pitch –
a muddy, snowy incline we were forced to traverse across. I
watched as the ground started to slide slowly as she moved
across it. There would be no stable foothold to be had, and this
was my Achilles' heel of climbing mountains – the precarious
sidehill maneuver with a giant drop-off below.

Legs wobbly beneath me, I got myself right into the thick of
it, one foot on solid ground behind, the other in the mud and
scree. I held on to the rock with my hands and tried to take
the next step, a step up onto the ridge. But I couldn't move. I
froze there, feeling my right foot starting to slide down, un-
willing to remove the left from its stable position to take the
step. I could feel it in my body, the fear starting to build up, the
mental paralysis beginning to set in. I called Julie's name in a
strained voice.

"I need help," I said, trying to keep my voice even, trying
to jam my foot even harder into the mud so it would hold. It
was hard to admit out loud, hard to say to the mountains, that
I had reached a spot I couldn't move from and would need
someone else's hand to pull me through.

Julie shrugged off her pack and leaned down, reaching her
hand out to me to use as a hold, to give me some sense of stability to swing my left foot up to where it needed to go. With a
deep breath, I was up on the ridge – we were out of the woods.

And when we stepped up onto the unusually flat, wide ridge that allowed the nervous energy in my body to begin to subside, we were nearly bowled over by the view that awaited us. Mount Moran and Leigh Canyon to the north, the Grand Teton itself to the south, and range beyond range of jagged mountains to the west. We kept turning around and around, not wanting to look at any one spot for too long in case we missed something, both of us shouting repeatedly about the astonishing beauty, the grandness and vastness and dizzying scale of everything around us. It filled us up all the way past the brim until the adrenaline, the gladness, the awe spilled over into the canyons below. And though of any hike we did during our stay in the Tetons, it had been easily the most miserable, the most frightening, the most challenging – it was also without question my favorite.

Sometimes you don't know what's waiting for you up above, up unrelenting switchbacks and precarious scree fields and snowfields in July. You can't see it from below, you can't know it until you've reached it, you can't fully understand how it will feel until you get there. And you can't get there if you stop when it gets hard. You can't get there if you let your fatigue and your weariness and your apathy get the better of you. The only way to get there, to get to that 360-degree view of mountains beyond mountains stacked on top of one another till they knock up against the horizon, is to keep moving. To keep pushing, to keep taking steps forward and telling yourself you can do it. Telling yourself you have to. Because often we struggle the most to get to the greatest things. Your feet may hurt, your legs may be tired, you may want to be anywhere but where you are, doing what you're doing, but none of those things should deter you from getting up every morning and climbing upward into all the glorious unimaginable beauty that awaits.

A Love Letter to Winter

It had been snowing all day and now it was dark, the air thick with falling flakes. The world was muffled and soft in the way it only is when it snows, and after dinner my dad started getting our coats and snow pants and boots on. We were little and an adventure outside in the dark seemed to swirl with added mystique. My dad threw the snowshoes into our silver Volvo station wagon, my brother and I hopped into the "back-back" – the third row of seats that faced backward – and we were off.

The car wound down the hill, skating across streets slick with snow, to the wooded golf course a few miles away. My dad helped us strap on our snowshoes and poles and headlamps, and we took off into the soft deep night.

We tromped through snow, my dad leading the way with his headlamp, watching fat flakes float down through the pine boughs, filling the atmosphere, landing on our rosy cheeks. We were the only ones out there in the cold quiet, walled off from the regular world by tall trees, transported to another dimension that only existed in green and white. This world was wildness and wonder and magic.

* * *

The world record for snow depth was measured on Mount Ibuki in the Japanese Alps in February of 1927. A whopping 465 inches, or nearly 39 feet, covered the spine of Honshu Island, where several factors create ideal conditions for heavy snowfall. Cold air from Siberia picks up moisture over the Sea of Japan and twirls in a perfect dance with northwest winds to nuke the mountains for several days at a time. Even now, the average annual snowfall tops 262 inches, and visitors can travel on shuttle buses through the Japanese "Snow Canyon," or Tateyama Kurobe Alpine Route, dwarfed by towering walls of tightly packed snow.

* * *

I grew up skiing at a small family-owned mountain in Maine, where lift lines were nonexistent and the T-bars outnumbered the chairlifts. We sang Dixie Chicks on the 12-minute ride up the ancient double chair and skied between each other's legs on the bunny slope and played endless games of bullshit and Egyptian rat screw on the long wooden tables in the lodge. We dropped our poles for the person behind us to catch on the T-bar and greeted the lifties by name and one-skied in the afternoons when we got bored of the trails we knew by heart.

After we were done for the day, the kids would steal trays from the cafeteria and take them outside while our parents drank pitchers of beer in the bar upstairs. The sky would paint itself in pastels and we'd swap our ski boots for Bean boots, running up the bunny hill with our trays to slide down the half-pipe, out of control and tipping over every few feet.

The evening air bit at our noses and mugs of hot chocolate called to us from the lodge, but we stayed out anyway, running back up the hill until we could feel our toes again. Launching ourselves downhill on things that weren't meant for snow travel numbed the cold. With our parents inside and everyone else packed up and gone for the day, we were kings and queens of this enchanted kingdom. When the light started to drain from the sky, turning the faraway peaks into silhouettes, the mountain was empty. It was ours.

* * *

The most dramatic cold snap on record in North America occurred in February of 1899, when the temperature in every single state in the Union dropped below zero. Typically balmy states like Florida reported record low temperatures of -2 degrees, while Montana clocked in at a bone-chilling -61 degrees. This weather event was so significant not merely because of the low temperatures recorded, but because of how widespread and far-reaching the effects were. It didn't isolate itself to regions in which cold normally reigns, but rather seeped into every part of the map, draping the entire United States in an impenetrable chill. A chill that left no doubt about what season it was, and about what that meant.

* * *

In high school we would toss our Nordic skis in the storage compartment underneath the bus and get shuttled over to the trail system 15 minutes away. Practices were spent doing long laps through the woods and working on our poling and gliding technique and occasionally tromping off trail to hide in the trees while our coaches were elsewhere. We learned to stagger our pole plant on steep uphills and pole every step on wide-open flats to keep our weight centered over our boots and glide as long as we could on each foot. We did sprints and relays and felt our lungs bursting with cold air.

Nordic skiing was hard work, but there was a satisfying rhythm to it, a gracefulness that came with years of practice and trying to go fast. With attention and carefully curated muscle memory, it started to feel a little like flying. Steadily pushing up hills, gliding across the flats and stepping to the beat around corners as we careened downhill. It created a warmth inside of us that belied the frigid temperatures of the winter months.

In the winter it got dark between 4:00 and 4:30 in the afternoon, and we would often find ourselves racing the fading sun back to the parking lot. The light would drop behind the bare spindly trees, and we'd be left with the pale after-blue as we piled onto the bus, sweaty and rosy-cheeked. We sat with our knees up on the seat in front of us, talking to each other across the aisles, feeling that warmth you do when you get into the car and relax after a long afternoon outside in the cold. More than anything else in high school, ski team felt like home. And it was then I began to equate winter with happiness.

* * *

A snow crystal begins its journey as water vapor. It turns directly into ice when the temperature is at or below 32 degrees Fahrenheit, and it falls to the earth. All snow crystals have six arms but are all unique depending on the temperature and humidity present during their creation. Some have longer needle arms, some have flat wide arms and still others have thinner branching arms. It all depends on the temperatures and humidities they experience. Even when they fall in silent breathtaking unison, each snow crystal is distinct because each one takes a slightly variant path as they tumble through the atmosphere. Each one takes its own journey; finds its own way down.

* * *

I spent most of my college winters bundled up in a knee-length down coat, walking between classes as quickly as possible in Chicago. Snow was pushed to the side and turned brown in hours, just something getting in everyone's way. I had moved to the city and spent far more time in heels than I did in ski boots. For winter break my senior year, I got on a plane and headed to Park City, Utah, where several hundred of my classmates and I would spend the week drinking and skiing in the mountains.

One of my roommates was mostly interested in hanging out, so she and I had split the cost of the trip, which left her with a bed and me with lift tickets. I would spend the week sleeping on the floor, getting up early to ski, and she passed the days eating weed brownies and going ice-skating. A true win-win.

After skiing we would shower and put on flannel and vests and take the shuttle to a bar in town, where we would order whiskey that hadn't been watered down by the Mormons. The bar was all hardwood, with twinkle lights and old ski paraphernalia everywhere. It was strange that being in a place I'd never been felt like coming home, but it did. I couldn't know then that later my life would be more like this week than anything else I was doing in the city. That with the exception of the pre-après shower, I would spend a large portion of my 20s like this – in mountain bars after a long day on the snow, drinking whiskey and watching the light drain from the sky.

The future familiarity of the situation seemed to saturate

itself backward to the present, and I found myself feeling a strange draw to stay there. I pulled my drink off the hardwood bar, looked around the room, soft with warm light, and out at the snowy street outside, and for a moment felt like a version of myself I once was, and one day would be again.

* * *

Twenty of the warmest years on record have occurred since 1981. The ten warmest years on record have occurred in the last 12. The earth has experienced cycles of glacial advance and retreat, but it is widely accepted by the scientific community that humans are, in fact, causing global climate change on a large scale. Carbon dioxide traps heat in the atmosphere, contributing to a spike in average global temperatures. Evidence of this change is clear in rising sea levels, warming oceans, shrinking ice sheets, glacial retreat, extreme weather events and reduced snow cover. In September 2016, global levels of carbon dioxide finally crossed the significant 400-parts-per-million threshold. The last time the earth had a level of CO_2 this high, there were no humans around to witness it.

* * *

When I was 22 I did a semester in New Zealand with the National Outdoor Leadership School (NOLS). On the month-long mountaineering section, it snowed so hard the helicopter couldn't make it into the Ashburton Glacier valley for our re-supply. We were forced to stretch out the last of our food for another day, which resulted in my cook group eating a questionable concoction deemed "spice kit soup." Our instructors told us to conserve our energy and stay in the tent resting in the hopes that the weather would clear and the helicopter would make it in the next day.

The valley was vast and flat, and none of us had chosen to spend three months in the backcountry because we liked to lie around and do nothing. A few of us pulled our gaiters and camp shoes on and crept out of our snow-dusted tents into the great sprawling white.

We plodded around the valley, the surrounding mountains shrouded in clouds and snow, singing the few verses we remembered to songs and talking about our lives. We made it to the creek in the center of the valley, the smooth stones capped with white pillows, the icy water rushing along to its own beat. I stared at it, mesmerized, understanding fully for the first time that this creek would move exactly this way even if we didn't exist and never had.

We found a giant boulder in the middle of the valley and climbed up onto it, throwing our arms out and our heads back. The snow still fell rapidly and silently onto every inch of our calorie-deprived bodies. We weren't supposed to be out here, seeing this, and the landscape felt more expansive for it. We were impossibly tiny figures that barely registered. And yet we were here. We were in it. We were part of it.

* * *

In 2015 the Sierra Nevada saw only 5 percent of its typical annual snowpack – 5 percent. Rocks and trees that would normally be hibernating feet below the surface baked in the sun. Ski resorts opened late and closed early, or remained shut down entirely. Gone from the air was that cold white magic, the days when you woke up and ran to the window like a child, jumping up and down because there was a foot of fresh on the ground and because the floor was cold and you needed a pair of wool socks. The mountains stayed in their summer skin, and winter enthusiasts hoped it was a one-off. It was the driest winter in 1,200 years.

* * *

The snow had been coming down all night, and Colorado in late April was still in the thick of ski season. We traversed across the East Wall, the atmosphere still teeming with fresh falling flakes. We passed the gates to the first two bootpacks, the sounds of bona fide whoops of joy around us on all sides. We kept traversing right, nearly to the end of the resort boundary – legwork it seemed few skiers that day were willing to do.

The reward for our efforts was immediately apparent. We

were looking down several hundred feet of untracked powder, with no one behind or in front of us. Growing up back east, a pow day had consisted of any fresh snow to speak of, when the sun wasn't reflecting off the glare ice and blinding you. But out here it was real.

Within seconds of dropping in, I knew this line would be different from any other line I had ever skied. Where normally there was resistance, where your metal edges braced power-fully against the snow, carrying you in a wide arc across the hill, there was nothing. There was lightness and utter freedom. I was turning on clouds, sailing through what many seek but do not always find – bottomless blower. Inbounds.

I couldn't help it – I cried out. My own joy whoops were re-leased into the air, rife with snow. It was involuntary, it was the only thing left to do. When you suddenly found yourself fly-ing, there was no choice but to throw your head back in grate-ful incredulity. It took you back to a state of childlike wonder, back to the dark snowy woods on a weeknight. It was pure freedom.

* * *

You can feel it in the air, smell it, when the snow is coming. Even if it's not coming that day or even that week, it's palpable, what's about to be. The colors in the sky change, winter's pal-ette smoother and more muted than summer's. The windshield is fogged up when you get into the car in the morning, the air bites at your fingers and your nose. And when it comes, when it finally comes twirling down from the heavens, there is a fullness, a stillness, a quietness, akin to no other season.

We are all children when we look out a window and suddenly see the air outside filled with white. We are all children when we float on a pillow of cold smoke. We are all children when we slide down a mountain, the cold air pinching our cheeks pink. We are all children when we run inside at the end of the day, longing to wrap our numb fingers around a mug of something warm. We are all children when we step out into the chilly night to roll the trash cans to the end of the driveway, and stop, mesmerized by the falling flakes illuminated in the golden light of streetlamps.

The magic doesn't fade. And we can't let it.

How Can I Support You?

The sky was gray and the sea restless and we had just pulled up to a desolate beach somewhere in the Marlborough Sounds. I sat on a piece of driftwood with my head between my knees, taking belabored breaths in and out of my mouth, relishing the stillness of my current position. For weeks the water had been calm and impossibly blue, but today it tossed our kayaks about like playthings. My stomach had grown more and more uneasy until I'd fallen completely silent for fear of opening my mouth. My expedition mate Babalu had motioned for us all to pull ashore, telling me afterward he knew something must be wrong when I stopped talking.

Babalu, always attuned to the needs of those around him, had noticed something was wrong and given the signal for us to pull off the water to give me a chance to recover. While others explored the beach and took bathroom breaks, Babalu sat next to me and fed me his ration of snacks until I felt normal again.

During the first few days of our semester, our sea kayaking

instructors Ben and Sally had told us about Expedition Behavior, or EB, and how it's the backbone upon which any good trip rests. It means doing your share and then just that little bit more. It means thinking of others before yourself. It means asking if anyone needs their Nalgene filled and offering to carry the cast-iron fry bake in your pack for the day. It means waking up early to boil water for hot drinks and doing extra dishes. It means kicking painstakingly excellent steps for the people behind you across a steep snowfield and letting someone else have the last pull of peanut butter. It means being kind and giving and big-hearted.

Babalu was the one moving the kayaks up the beach in the rain when the tide came in, the one taking care of anyone who felt sick, the one waking up early to boil water, the one continuing to carry the heavy climbing rope, even when his knee was bothering him. He was the kind of person everyone wanted on their team.

Years after my NOLS semester, I found myself preparing to lead my own trip for Adventures Cross Country. After a night with little sleep, I stood in the office, struggling to complete a job chart that suddenly felt like a complicated algorithm from hell that would crush my soul before it was done. My co-leader David, at this point a relative stranger, came in from the other room and, after watching me scrunch my forehead up painfully trying to figure out whose turn it was next for cook crew, asked me a question that was staggering in its simplicity.

"How can I support you?"

I looked over at him, quite possibly with my jaw actually hanging open. *How can I support you.* It was so basic, and yet so unbelievable. It was a question that seemed to wrap you in its arms. It was unassuming, understated and yet so filled with kindness that I felt the stress of the task melt away. It was maybe the best question I had ever been asked. It was EB in a sentence.

On the first night of the trip I led around Northern California, a student pulled me aside to express her concern about the group dynamic. As is common at the very beginning of anything, she was feeling uncomfortable and craving a return to the familiarity of her regular life. I decided to try it – I asked her how I could support her, and I watched as her entire face changed. It was a magical question capable of making anyone feel held.

In the outdoors and in life we rarely accomplish anything alone. We are roped up, we lead and are led, we hold on to each other and we hold each other up. We cheer each other on, we put sunscreen on each other's backs, we keep each other warm at night. We need each other.

When you venture into the backcountry with people, you are inevitably and necessarily putting your trust in them and they in you. You are saying to each other that, if something goes wrong, if someone gets hurt, if unforeseen complications befall you, you will be there. That you will pull off the water and feed them snacks, that you will talk them through the hard parts, that if necessary you will stabilize their neck and check their c-spine, that you will dig them out of the snow. That you will support them in any and every way they need to be supported, and they will do the same for you.

Back in the frontcountry it's easier to forget about EB. It's easier to look at the person struggling with a job chart or homesickness or the copy machine or insecurity and let them handle it themselves. It's easier to do less than your share. They're not straddling a crevasse or buried in an avalanche or bleeding.

But imagine what would happen, imagine what kind of world we would live in, if we all asked how we could support each other, and then did it. Imagine how that would change our relationships and our lives.

BECOMING

When I signed up for my first ultra, I had never even run a marathon. I had actually said multiple times I would never run a marathon, because a half just seemed like a much less complicated distance. Less pain, less training – why push it? And yet, despite this, I found myself in a brewery in Denver in December with three women who, at the time, were relative strangers registering for a 50k in the Grand Canyon that spring.

I'd met them a few months before, doing another thing I thought I'd never do – showing up somewhere alone. I'd pulled into a gravel parking lot at a trailhead and walked up to a group of people I didn't know who also wanted to go on an evening trail run and drink beer afterward. I'd felt the stretch, the strangeness – the taut resistance you push past when you do something you're not quite ready for.

I felt instantly transported back to being an uncomfortable 17-year-old walking into parties I didn't feel I belonged at, surrounded by people who thrived there, by people who saw each other every weekend. I remembered walking down into carpeted basements, holding myself stiffly, staying close to the people I'd come with.

As I got older, I heard about these mythical creatures who would show up at places alone, who could fend for themselves. It seemed foreign and fascinating to me, this idea of feeling so confident and comfortable with yourself that you could show up somewhere by yourself, or interact independently with a bunch of people you didn't know while the people you came with were off somewhere else. I found myself wanting to be the kind of person who could do that.

It turns out there is a difference between wanting to be something and wanting to become something. Wanting to be something indicates a hope that somehow you will be struck by lightning and suddenly *be* that thing you wanted to be. Wouldn't it be nice if I were suddenly, somehow, more outgoing, more confident. Hoping to be something is passive, and passivity gets you nowhere.

Being is a state, and becoming is a process. And to be, you must become. Becoming requires work. Becoming requires action. Becoming means deciding you're going to achieve something and taking real quantifiable steps in that direction.

When I was 24 I got into graduate school and moved to Colorado, where I knew practically no one. I spent the first six months pining for Maine, where I'd left my life, where I always had someone to show up with and people to talk to.

Here, I had to work. Here, I had to step outside of that comfort if I wanted to find my people. If I wanted to become the person I wanted to be. So one night I decided to show up at a trailhead parking lot where a running group was meeting up to run and drink beer afterward.

I could hear all the familiar excuses to not go banging their fists in my head, a million reasons to turn the car around. But somewhere else in my head was the voice of the person I wanted to be, the person I had yet to become. Somewhere was the voice that told me the only way to become the kind of person who felt comfortable showing up places alone was to show up places alone.

So I showed up. Ultimately, I parked my car, walked up to a circle of people with running clothes on and introduced myself. I ended up running five miles on beautiful trails and talking to interesting people and going home feeling like I'd *done* something. I showed up somewhere alone and ran up hills and I was okay. I had taken a step in the direction of becoming the person I wanted to be.

And the thing about taking that first step is that you can use it to take the rest of them. You've already done it once. So when the next opportunity presents itself to step, you can look back and remember that first trail run. Little by little, you walk your way there.

A few weeks later, I went to an avalanche awareness night

with two of the women I'd met at that first run. There was free beer and a raffle and a balloon pit for beacon practice and a giant poster wall where you could write your goals in Sharpie. I picked two and wrote them in big letters: "ski 20 days and run a 50k."

I wanted to be the kind of person who ran uphill. I wanted to be the kind of person who had excellent foot placement on rock and dirt. I wanted to be the kind of person who could go for hours. I wanted to be the kind of person who did ultras.

If there is something you want to be, you must become it, step by step. You cannot wake up one day with no effort and find yourself an ultrarunner. You must become an ultrarunner a little bit every single day, until that is what you are. Until the process has created the state.

The first step to becoming an ultrarunner was to sign up for an ultra, which we did a few weeks later. We ordered IPAs and laughed nervously and plunked down the entrance fees for a 50k. We were really in it now.

We started slow, running 10 miles, 12 miles, 14 miles. I bought better shoes and a hydration vest and sleeves of Shot Bloks. I read articles about nutrition and recovery and form.

The four of us started talking about our lives and our struggles and our relationships and our dreams, and, as the miles passed, the women I'd been intimidated to talk to in a parking lot when I first met them were now my people.

And then we put in bigger days, running 18 miles, 20 miles, 22 miles. The closer we got to race day, the more things started to shift. The numbers remained the same, but what they meant began to change. Suddenly, any run in the single digits was short, and previously unattainable distances were weekend plans. Saying something is impossible is a great way to get out of having to try. These distances might have remained unattainable, if I'd decided to let them. If I hadn't woken up, laced up my shoes and just done it.

Before I knew it, race day was upon us. We arrived at the Grand Canyon to a cold snap and four inches of fresh snow on the ground. The course had been changed from an A to B along the rim of the Grand Canyon to an out-and-back to the rim, and now it would be four miles longer. But here we were, poised to run 36 miles, poised to become the people we had set out to be.

We spent the next nine hours running and walking, eating and hydrating, chatting and retreating into our own heads. And before I knew it, I had entered into this alternate state, the state you get into when you've been running for multiple hours and you sort of forget what it feels like to not be moving forward. The running is just your reality; it's what you came here to do.

When we hit mile 30 and should have been close to done, I became intimately acquainted with a place endurance athletes know well: the pain cave. You feel like a slightly compromised human, like lying down on the side of the trail, like you're not sure you're still all there. You put on James Brown to get you to the last aid station without giving in to the weirdness, you stop bothering to hide behind things to pee, you keep moving because you know that's what you came here to do.

But experiencing these things, this discomfort, these trials, is exactly what ultrarunners do. And so, as we were suffering, and wishing we were done, and eating handfuls of potato chips and gummy bears, we were also becoming.

By late afternoon, the snow had melted and turned into ankle-deep mud and the light was fading, and then before I knew it I was cresting the final hill down to the finish. I was struck by this overwhelming, contradictory, simultaneous feeling of disbelief and triumph. This feeling that I always knew I could do this, and yet also shock that I had actually done it. I crossed the line with happy tears running onto my shoulders and wings in my heart.

To be you must become, and to become you must move. To become you must get up and stand up and show up and live up. It is the simplest and the most difficult thing, because you are the one solely responsible for doing it.

If you want to be someone who is brave, live with courage. If you want to be someone who is honest, tell the truth. If you want to be someone who is strong, do something that requires strength. Do those things and therefore become the kind of person who would do them. Wishing or aspiring to be a certain way does nothing. You must act. You must act that way until you are that way.

And, little by little, with repetitive action stirred on by the echoes of those initial actions, you become habitually brave or honest or strong. You become someone who can walk into a party alone or run an ultramarathon. You become that way because you stand up and choose to be that way, over and over.

Tolerance for Uncertainty and Adversity

It was four in the morning, it was sideways sleeting and the tent pole cup was broken. I stood huddled in my rain gear, aiming my headlamp down at my tent mate and my instructor who were lying sideways on the icy snow, trying to speedy-stitch the stirrup back to the tent body before they lost all dexterity in their hands. It was four in the morning and I was supposed to be snuggled up in my sleeping bag inside the tent, but instead I was outside getting pelted with rain on the side of a snowy mountain, the blackness around me increasing the sense of being in the absolute middle of nowhere. It was at this particular moment I began to question what the hell it was I was doing there, why someone would intentionally volunteer to put themselves in this kind of situation, and when were we going to be able to crawl back into the warm(ish) dry(ish) tent? The answers to the first two questions seemed uncertain, and the answer to the third was not until we had fixed the tent.

We had been out in the backcountry of New Zealand for over a month, and yet this was the first moment I'd experienced that had been such a forcible reminder of who the boss was out here. If slanting, freezing rain and gigantic wind gusts hit your tent all night, no one was going to call it off. No one was going to spare you. No one was going to fix it for you while you rolled over and went back to sleep. You had to wake up, put on your rain pants and rain jacket and fix the tent yourself – lest you all be blown off the mountain when the tent poles snapped.

We had spent the hours leading up to the fateful tent-pole-cup disaster in a state of bleary-eyed flux between trying to fall back to sleep and snapping upright to brace the tent poles when a gust shot over the mountains and ripped its way through the valley we were camped in. The intensity of the volume of the wind shaking the tent and the pressure of the walls pushing down onto your shoulders and neck seemed almost too great to be believed. The pitifulness of the tent in the face of the power of the wind was so absurd it would eventually become funny, but right then we just braced, lay back down, braced, lay back down, and braced, in bewildered, exhausted silence.

I told this story four years later while driving up to do a ten-mile ski tour in the Indian Peaks Wilderness in Colorado. I was with my friend Lindsay, who would be my partner for the Grand Traverse – a 40-mile overnight ski mountaineering race from Crested Butte to Aspen – a few months later. That day's tour would be our first big training day for the race, and we were discussing all of the anticipated challenges. Food and water freezing, losing feeling in our hands when transitioning our setups from uphill to downhill mode, bonking, being in our boots for 15 hours – the list wound on longer than the road taking us into the mountains.

The Grand Traverse was your textbook sufferfest – a long arduous journey in adverse conditions. Luckily, Lindsay and I were no strangers to sufferfests. She talked about summiting Mount Katahdin, Maine's tallest peak, in the winter when she was 15, and completing a Hut Traverse – a 24-hour, 49-mile speed hike connecting all the Appalachian Mountain Club's high mountain huts, with a whopping 17,000 feet of elevation gain.

My mind flashed to the three months I'd spent on the South Island, sea kayaking against a three-knot current in the driving rain in the Marlborough Sounds, putting on frozen boots morning after morning in the Arrowsmiths, tucking wet socks into my puffy coat at night to dry them out, staying up all night to prevent 120 km/h winds from ripping down the tent, spending four hours hacking out a glacier camp after postholing uphill all day.

There were so many moments during my three months in

the wilderness when I was cold, wet, hungry, tired, frustrated, confused, in pain and afraid. And in many cases more than one of those at once. Because those are inevitabilities of outdoor living. You are out in the elements, and you will have to face them. And yet I still count those three months among the best of my life.

My time in the New Zealand backcountry taught me many things. How to light a stove, how to self-arrest with an ice axe, how to make a splint out of sticks or a trekking pole, how to triangulate my location with a map and compass – but most importantly it taught me how to suffer well. How to feel cold, wet, hungry, tired, frustrated, confused, in pain and afraid, and how to keep going. How to push through those things to accomplish the objective. How to take care of yourself to avoid feeling some of those ways if you could. How to take care of others in the same situation. How to somehow tuck yourself into your sleeping bag full of wet clothes at the end of a long day and smile, despite all the reasons not to.

Because woven within the suffering were moments of grace so intense, so heart-blindingly incredible, that you would never stop coming back for more. Even when it hurt. After the early wake-up call, the frozen boots and the hours of postholing was the sunrise summit. When it was raining in your face and you were paddling as hard as you could against the current and you couldn't see anything, it turned out the only thing to do was laugh at the absurdity of life. When the ultra-marathon ended up being 36 miles instead of 32, tears of joy welled up in your chest when you rounded the last hill toward the finish line and realized you'd actually done it. And so it became clear that with that kind of suffering came a singular kind of beauty.

As Lindsay and I trudged through the snow in single-digit weather, the wind howling in our faces, our fingers numb and our snacks frozen, I felt a strange sort of familiarity with it all. The cold, the hunger, the exhaustion. The small part of me asking why the hell I was out here.

I already knew how to do this. I already knew how to dig deep.

I already knew that only those who were willing to wade through the suffering with a smile in their hearts would see the splendor of the mountaintop.

NOLS has an entire leadership principle dedicated to handling these kinds of circumstances: Tolerance for Uncertainty and Adversity. And cultivating a talent for it will alter what you believe is possible.

No matter how dark the night, or deep the snow, your legs will get you there, if your mind believes they can.

Everything Counts

I remember sitting on the plane to New Zealand with the distinct feeling this was the beginning of the rest of it, the beginning of everything that came after the linear formula of youth. I was 22 and freshly out of college, on the brink of a one-of-a-kind year of meandering. I was sitting alone in the middle seat, pointed toward a side of the world I'd never been before, away from everything I had known up until that moment. The tingle of giddy excitement and anxious terror that heralds adventure shot up through fingers as I gripped the armrest, watching Boston disappear below me. It was all out there, waiting. Yet to be.

I remembered this moment viscerally flying back to the United States from Chile almost a year later, how it had felt to be on the verge. On the verge of everything that had just happened. It felt like the end in some strange way, though of course it wasn't. It was the end of the first year, maybe, but as always things would keep moving and something else would be next. I had that strange feeling I often get that the time that had passed and the things that had happened between the two flights couldn't possibly map onto each other. I remembered that flight to Auckland like I had just gotten off it, and yet thinking of everything that had occurred between then and now made it seem like a distant memory.

I remember one afternoon in New Zealand when we were stranded at an organic farm in the Marlborough Sounds for a few days, and, after a false-start launch delayed by surly looking storm clouds, we all took a hike around the cove. The trail was damp from days of rain and surrounded by dark heavy pines and Justine was talking about Japhy, the main character from Jack Kerouac's *The Dharma Bums*, a book she tried to read at least once a year. We walked back to the large sheep barn we were taking shelter in and Justine realized she'd lost her camera. She had insisted on going back for it alone, even though it was a long walk and it had started to rain, and not until months later, when I met Japhy on the pages of *The Dharma Bums*, did I understand why Justine came back a while later from her solitary walk, soaking wet and smiling so big it filled the entire barn.

I remember sitting in a hostel in Argentina, using my Speedy Stitcher to do surgery on the fraying back of my ever-present travel companion, Bag of Wonders. My friend Marielle shook her head at me and told me to just buy a new purse while I tried to recall the steps Colt had taught me after having to repair his backpack hip strap and various parts of our tent in the Arrowsmiths. I remembered his tall frame hunched over in our tent, parked on the banks of a river, making sure each stitch was even, slipping into his goofy seamstress alter ego to amuse Connor and me while we tried to put away our third bowls of cold rice. I remember looking down at my own stitches on Bag of Wonders and knowing I was light years away from matching Colt's handiwork, but that at the very least I was able to prevent my valuables from falling to the sidewalk through a fist-sized hole in the bag's lining.

I remember feeling nervous but capable in Chile when my head teacher asked me to teach 90-minute classes alone to a group of ten students from each grade instead of assistant teaching in class with her like I'd been told I was going to. I thought of leading the girls' Nordic ski team in my hometown on a warm-up run of the course and going over technique tips and race strategy. I remember having the same feeling of purpose, of exhaustion but satisfaction, in the classroom and on the trails. I remember thinking that, no matter where they grow up and what they're doing, middle school kids are essentially the same – all a little unsure of themselves and funnier than they realize.

I remember sitting on my bed in my house my senior year of college, spiraling into a panic while everyone I knew put on suits and went to career fairs and practiced case studies, feeling like I was suddenly being thrust into something I hadn't prepared for and didn't want. Why hadn't I gotten internships during college summers? Why didn't I own a power suit? Was this all there was after graduation?

I remember sitting in an international phone booth in Chile, interviewing for a job in a backcountry hut that didn't require a suit or heels, calling effortlessly on my past experiences to answer questions and realizing everything I'd done in the past had counted, had led me to this exact spot, had, in fact, better prepared me for this job than any internship could have.

I remember standing outside in the driving rain at four in the morning at our snow camp with Colt and Jared, trying to fix our tent so it wouldn't be claimed by the angry winds. I remember standing in my driveway as a light snow fell in December and feeling like I didn't want to or know how to go inside. I remember yelling and crying as my parents and I tried to figure out how this whole living-at-home-after-college thing was going to work. I remember getting dropped off at a random street corner in 90-degree Calama, Chile, with Marielle after a creepy, sleepless overnight bus ride and having no idea where the bus terminal was. I remember spending four hours waiting in the cramped, noisy *extranjería* in Santiago, waiting to pay a fine for my visa. I remember checking my email one day at school in Copiapó and discovering, in the same minute and a half, that my Great-Aunt Angela had died and I hadn't gotten a job I'd interviewed for. I remember having a panic my last week in Chile that I was making a huge mistake by leaving. I remember looking at my flight confirmation in the airport in Santiago as I was leaving and realizing I'd missed my flight and would need to dig into all of my savings to get myself home. I remember feeling miserable, confused, frustrated, scared, disappointed and lost. I remember feeling maybe I had made a mistake in choosing this uncertain, non-linear path, and wouldn't it be easier if I were just living in an apartment with a full-time job somewhere.

I remember creeping out of my tent in the early morning, clutching my sleeping bag to watch the sunrise over Lake Ohau with Justine and Colt and Babalu, I remember the overflowing pride as my middle school skiers crossed the finish line at their state meet, I remember feeling like I'd been punched in the gut when Marielle and I rounded a corner in Glacier National Park in Patagonia and were suddenly staring up at Monte Fitz Roy, I remember laughing until my jaw hurt playing the chair game with my students in class, I remember hiking to the top of one of the many mountains surrounding Copiapó with Natalie and Diego, gazing out over the sprawling Atacama Desert. I remember feeling exhilarated, awestruck, joyful, accomplished, fulfilled, lucky. I remember feeling every single step of the way that I was in the right place, doing the right thing.

I remember walking along the Presidential Ridge in the White Mountains with Justine a year after we'd left New Zealand, wondering about which steps to take and what came next. I'd sometimes find myself getting caught in this need to figure out which decision was the "right" one, and that was where I found myself in that particular moment. In a few days fall hut season would end and I would make the final descent from my home on Mount Washington and into uncertainty. Were we on the right path? Should we have done things differently? Moving our bodies through a large boulder field, we shook our heads. Every decision we'd made in our lives, big or small, had led us here, to this moment in the mountains. And whether or not I knew they were right or wrong at the time, I'd made them deliberately. I'd made them with my eyes open, and they'd brought me through all the experiences that, stacked up on top of each other, created the person I was, a person I wouldn't take back.

I remember while in Chile in 2011 reading a book called *Even Silence Has an End*, by kidnapped 1990s Colombian political candidate Ingrid Betancourt. Held captive in the jungle by guerilla forces for six years, she used her prior knowledge of needlepoint to keep from losing her grip on reality. She wrote, "Now I realized that life supplies us with everything we need for the journey. Everything I had acquired either actively or passively, everything I had learned either voluntarily or by osmosis, was coming back to me as the real riches of my life."

I remember realizing everything counts, that everything we do somehow contributes to who we are as people, to what we do and where we go and who we are next. That what we do inherently informs what we do next, that we cannot stop everything around us from shaping not only our present experience but also our future experiences. If we do things for the right reasons, for reasons that feel true and organic and necessary, those things will naturally lead us to the next right thing. Everything builds off everything else. Nothing we do mindfully is useless or pointless.

I remember sitting on the chair on the back patio of my house in Copiapó reading *The Dharma Bums* before the sandy mountains that looked blue in the morning light, and the character Ray saying, "I saw that my life was a vast glowing empty page and I could do anything I wanted." I remember smiling and knowing it had been true all year and it was still true now, looking forward.

For the Love of the Tour

Lindsay and I had been touring for four hours and had yet to rip skins. Even when we did, it would be to shred several miles of hard-packed fire road at a 5 percent grade. Not exactly what anyone would refer to as the good stuff.

Everyone has different reasons for attaching sticky carpets to the bottoms of their skis and heading uphill. For some, touring is simply a way to access backcountry terrain that's cheaper than hiring a heli. For others, it's a workout – a quick tour at the beginning or end of a resort day, or a way to stay fit during ultrarunning's off-season. Then there are those who seek out the romance of human-powered adventure, who find beauty in the quiet promise of a smooth skin track through an otherwise untouched landscape.

But today we fell into none of those categories. We were setting out on a 15-mile mission up the unmaintained road to Mount Evans on Colorado's Front Range that would involve crunching across wind-scoured Styrofoam to avoid the bits of road left exposed by the sun, and hardly any turns to speak of.

We were training for the Grand Traverse, and the goal was just to put down a bunch of miles on skis.

Touring takes skiing back to its simplest roots – a means of traveling across a snowy topography in a more efficient manner. It's all about the rhythmic grace of each footstep, about passing hours out in the mountains, about feeling the steady hum of your heartbeat and the satisfied tiredness at the end of the day.

You pull on your boots, smooth your skins onto your skis, click your toes into your bindings and settle into that organic cadence of putting one foot in front of the other. It is a kind of peace – a cold, hushed meditation—a way of passing through the wilderness that carries a certain humility.

There's a photo on the wall of my parents' house of two of my Swedish ancestors in the 1880s. They're standing outside a wooden cabin hung with icicles, wearing wool coats and pants, fur hats and touring gear. Wooden skis, wooden poles, leather boots, leather strap bindings. They are carrying packs and appear to be about to set off on an expedition. Many generations removed from any kind of meaningful cultural heritage, I look at this photo and feel a connection to my roots. I feel it in my blood when I'm out in the cold skinning, a rhythm that seems to have been in me since before I was born, something that echoes back into snowy trees of the distant past.

It was that ancient tempo, the quiet shush of skis on snow,

that pulsed in time with our hearts as we logged each mile. We settled into it, a beat that seemed to extend beyond us, beyond that moment and that place, and into a collective forward motion. To the tune of this drummer we carried on, merely for the sake of doing so.

Lindsay and I hadn't signed up for the Grand Traverse because we were trying to go particularly fast. We would be satisfied if we made it to the checkpoints before the cutoff and to the finish in time to have a victory burger and watch the sunset. I liked to think of it as multi-hour adventure, a creative and challenging way to get from Crested Butte to Aspen.

We were doing it because we were the kind of people who liked to be outside and have skis on our feet and push ourselves to do things we previously thought we could not. We were doing it because, since the dawn of time, humans have felt the pull of setting off into the great wide open and seeing what was there. We were doing it because at the end of a 15-mile slog we exchanged multiple exuberant high fives, laughed about who had eaten a weirder combination of pocket snacks and let the internal buzz of a great day in the mountains flow through our bodies and reverberate out into the wilderness.

The success of any outdoor mission is determined by its purpose. Any endeavor, depending on the objective of the undertakers, can be deemed worthwhile. The fire road wasn't a dreamy skin track through deep powder or over a majestic ridgeline, but the magic was still there. We were still going out into the snow on our own two feet, with mountains sprawled out all around us. The value was inherent in the movement itself.

Going Alone

It was a bright, clear, cold morning in early September and the Presidential Ridge, already flecked with ice, was sprawling out for miles on either side of me. I was 23 and working at Lakes of the Clouds, one of the Appalachian Mountain Club's backcountry huts in the White Mountains of New Hampshire. Madison was the next hut over, a 6.8-mile journey past Mounts Washington, Jefferson and Adams, through boulder fields, up and over countless rolling inclines. I had the time between serving breakfast to guests at 9:00 and serving them dinner at 5:00 to hike as far as I could and back, and today I had my sights set on traversing the northern end of the ridge – solo.

I had been running alone for years, but this would be the first multi-hour hike I would attempt without companions. It began as something done out of necessity – my coworkers were stuck inside cooking and manning the front desk – but I quickly realized hiking alone was actually this energizing, clarifying, amazing thing.

It was exhilarating, to be alone in the hugeness of it, of the wide granite ridge, the mountains rolling out over the horizon in blues and greens, the clear sky spreading itself overhead. There was nothing but me and the rhythm of my feet, the feeling of my muscles working, the clear air coursing through my being. It was magic, like someone had pulled back a curtain and presented me with this thing, this amazing energy I had never tapped into while hiking in groups.

My pace was unhindered. I didn't have to wait for others to de-layer or grab a snack. I could stop when I wanted to take pictures without having to worry about holding anyone up. I felt like I could process what I was seeing better in the silence, without chatter or other people's perceptions or distractions getting in the way. I tapped into a rhythm and rode it all the way along the ridge and back, and when I returned to the hut just in time to serve dinner, I felt recharged and energized in a way I never had before.

What was it? What was it about staring out at mountains for as far as your eyes could see, with no purpose except to run your feet over as much of them as you could? About just being a tiny human out in the middle of all of it, without music or conversation or anything to cloud the connection between you and the ancient elemental earth?

When I moved to Colorado, I was itching to explore every rocky corner and forgotten alpine lake of the Front Range but had not yet met anyone willing to wake up before dawn on a weekend to drive almost two hours to hike. I contemplated the options: staying home until I could find adventure buddies to accompany me into the wilderness, or going it alone – setting out for a trail I'd never been to by myself to chase the hit of mountain high I craved.

It soon became clear the pull was too great to ignore, so I began venturing out – driving long hours and hiking long days by myself. I saw crystalline lakes in Rocky Mountain National Park and thick coniferous forests outside Boulder and rolling fields of wildflowers in Crested Butte and herds of fleecy mountain goats in Summit County. I sometimes hiked quickly and without pause. I sometimes stopped for minutes at a time to stare up at towering rock walls. I consciously noticed the sun on my face and sat at summits for longer than most people want to. I pushed myself up switchbacks and steeps harder and faster than I thought I could. I worked through problems in my head, or I turned off my thoughts completely. I had to route find and make decisions and rely on myself. I came home feeling energized and bright-eyed and full.

There is a stigma with this, especially as a woman – one I came up against constantly when anyone found out I regularly hiked alone. I would be recounting something I'd seen or a place I'd been and people would default to asking me who I'd done it with. When I answered I'd been by myself, there was this unspoken sense of pity, that I couldn't find anyone to go with and therefore must have been lonely and resentful the entire time.

The other piece is you-shouldn't-be-going-out-into-the-wilderness-alone-as-a-lady. The piece that even as an adult prevented me from mentioning most of my excursions to my parents, that got me nervous looks or misguided advice that maybe I should take a man with me when I go out. This sense that doing anything independently as a female is ill-advised; that men can venture out alone as much as they want, but that we should wait until we have someone to protect us.

There is inherent risk, of course, in hiking alone. That can apply to any gender, but it's all about mitigation. Every time I leave the house, I text the GPS coordinates, trail description and trailhead directions to my roommate so someone knows where I am if there is no reception. I carry the ten essentials with me. I make sure to slow down and assess situations when the risks outweigh the benefits (resulting in several sprinting-back-down-the-mountain episodes just before summer thunderstorms hit).

But the possible risks shouldn't stop you from seeking the imminent beauty, the impending adventure. I wouldn't have seen all I've seen, wouldn't have connected so fully with the environment around me in my new home, wouldn't have gotten to know myself in the same way if I'd let the fact that I'm a woman alone stop me from going out into the wild.

Because the reality is there are too many heart-stopping, soul-filling corners out there waiting to be explored that women shouldn't have to wait for anyone else to get after. And maybe it's even more than that – maybe this solitude should be intentionally sought, should be treated as an opportunity to recharge and connect with yourself and your universe in a way that can only be achieved when it's just you and the mountains and the trees and the sky.

Lean In

It was March at Hatcher Pass in the Talkeetnas. I'd arrived in Alaska just the day before and my legs were already wobbly from bootpacking up and skiing the Lost Couloir earlier that morning. Our second line involved skinning up a steep, thinly covered pitch and then along a narrow ridge, trying to keep our skins on as long as we could. The angle required frequent switchbacking, and the slick, grainy snow underfoot made getting an edge in a grueling task. Every time my ski slipped out from under me I risked falling, and my entire body would go tingly with adrenaline and fear. I would freeze for a few seconds, trying to stabilize myself and catch my breath before I tried to place my foot again.

One of the most important things you can do on skis is keep your weight forward. Whether it's charging down a steep trail or cranking on a groomer or striding up the skin track, for the sailing to be smooth, you must angle your body in the direction you are moving. When I was learning to downhill race as a kid, they would tell us to make sure we could feel our shins pressing against the insides of our ski boots and warn us about "getting in the back seat." On the Nordic trails as a coach many years later, I instructed my athletes to center their weight over their bindings to properly set their classic wax on the uphill so their skis wouldn't slip out from under them. And I realized again the importance of keeping your weight forward when skinning up steep, icy switchbacks in the Alaskan backcountry, knowing if I leaned back even for a second, I could lose my footing.

It seems like a simple concept physically – to keep your weight forward – and it is. Physically, it is simple. But skiing, like most outdoor sports, is far from being a purely physical pursuit. Our brains get involved – our thoughts, our emotions and, most importantly, our fears. Fear is what gets us in the back seat. Fear is what causes us to slip backward. Fear – even at a subconscious, nearly undetectable level.

When something scares us, it is an instinctual reaction to back away. To move ourselves in the opposite direction of the thing we fear. To try to distance our bodies from the source of the anxiety. It is the flight response, but it doesn't necessarily mean we will actually remove ourselves from the situation or run away. It may just mean an ever so slight weight shift in the direction opposite of the one we need to go.

Each time it was time to end one switchback and begin another, we had to change directions to flip our skis and our bodies 180 degrees to begin slowly gaining elevation facing the other way. Doing this on trails while running and hiking is simple, but on skis it was suddenly a far more harrowing task. It involved facing backward down the mountain and balancing all our weight on one ski as we moved the other, trusting that one edge with our entire position on the side of the mountain. When I was nervous, when I wasn't confident in the placement of my edge in the snow, that was when the ski would slip and I would be forced to try to catch myself with my other ski or my poles. I wasn't driving forward, placing all of my strength and faith in myself squarely over my foot, so I was slipping backward, in the direction I had the weight of my body.

It happens when there is an increase in speed or a particularly challenging bit of terrain. It happens to racers trying to wrangle themselves through gates on an icy pitch, and it happens to free skiers trying to navigate steeps, and it happens to new skiers who are not yet confident in their own abilities. There is this almost unconscious shift backward, away from the speed, away from the steepness, away from the momentum and the gravity. Somehow our bodies think we are protecting ourselves – that we're making the situation safer.

But the result of leaning back on skis is the opposite of what your body's primal instinct thinks it will be. When you lean back, you take pressure off the front of your boots and you relinquish a certain amount of control over your skis.

And when you're already on terrain or at a speed where you feel uncomfortable or scared, by reducing your control over your skis you are actually putting yourself in more danger and increasing the likelihood of causing exactly what you feared to happen. When you are going uphill, leaning back will cause you to go in the direction opposite of the one you want – backward.

It's our instinct. It's an attempt at self-preservation. But what our bodies don't account for is that launching ourselves fully in the direction of what we fear is actually what will yield the best results. Actually thrusting forward, flowing with gravity, leaning into the momentum – that is how we must get up or down the mountain, and how we must attack our fears.

After a few slips that led me to pause for minutes at a time, clinging to my points of contact and breathing intentionally until I trusted my limbs again, it started echoing in my mind what I would tell the skiers on my Nordic team when they were going uphill on classic skis. Skinning on alpine touring skis wasn't all that different from classic skiing, except that skins were used for traction instead of kick wax. My weight, I realized, was not centered over the foot I was planting with. I was nervous, I didn't trust myself, and my upper body was leaning back as a result, throwing off everything I was doing. To get where I wanted to go, to move past the fear, I had to lean into the hill and drive my skis forward with confidence.

Confidence that would ensure good foot placement and secure my position on the skin track.

Fear can create a positive feedback loop. We are afraid, so we shrink and further invite the thing that scares us to occur. To beat the fear, to give ourselves a fighting chance at realizing the best possible outcome, we have to go all in and face it. Because we are not afraid of the speed. We are not afraid of the steepness. We are not afraid of the angles or the snowpack. We are afraid of what might happen to us. If we fail, if we falter. That is what drives our weight back, what causes our bodies to retreat.

But to change that feedback loop into a positive one, all we need to do is shift our weight forward. All we need to do is charge confidently in the direction we want to go, even if it makes us afraid. All we have to do is lean in.

Will You Do It Later, or Will You Do It Now?

In the middle of the night in New Zealand, I sprung awake, shaken from the kind of deep sleep you can only get when you've walked up and down mountains all day. I lay frozen in place, knowing exactly what was happening and wishing with all my might it wasn't. It was an inevitability of living life outside, something to be dreaded but not always avoided. Perhaps if I lay perfectly still, it would go away. Perhaps I could just fall peacefully back to sleep as if nothing had ever happened.

This happens sometimes – we freeze. We know what's happening and we try to convince ourselves it's not. We try to pretend we're making it all up in our heads, that, in fact, everything is fine as it has been. We try to go about business as usual because it's easier that way – because it doesn't involve disrupting the status quo, or looking something in the face that makes our stomachs turn.

But it was an unavoidable reality – I had to pee.

I went through the next few minutes in my head as I lay in my sleeping bag, unmoving and irritated with my poorly exe- cuted intentional nighttime dehydration strategy. A full ther- mos of hot chocolate, Highland? Really?

I would try to unzip my sleeping bag, and because the zipper was messed up, it would take minutes of vigorous and precise tugging to free myself from my synthetic down prison. Every part of my body was touching one or two other people's bod- ies in our five-people-to-a-four-person-tent-spoon-train situ- ation, so they would wake up. I would instantly be the asshole who broke the strict no-hot-drinks-after-8-p.m. rule.

I'd have to leave the warm comfort of my sleeping bag and crawl over at least two people to get to the vestibule, where I'd have to put on all my rain gear because it was sideways sleet- ing outside. Then the getting out of the tent. More zippers. So many zippers. Had someone invented a zipper silencer yet?

I would have to walk a respectable distance away from the tent in said sideways sleet and pull my pants down in the 40-degree weather and pee. And then I would have to repeat the entire beginning of the process in reverse.

I was exhausted just thinking about it. Maybe if I lay in just the right way, I wouldn't have to pee. Maybe it would just go away if I waited it out. Maybe I'd be so tired I'd just magic- ally fall back to sleep. Maybe I should just throw up my hands and pee in my sleeping bag. Anything seemed better than the veritable odyssey of getting out of the tent in the middle of the night.

For a straight half hour, I lay there, debating whether or not I would get up. Why had this horrible evil befallen me? What had I ever done to deserve this? Why did people even have to pee anyway? I thought back to my expedition mate Justine's wish for a backcountry power to vicariously pee through someone else, and I fully realized what a genius she truly was.

There will always be things we don't want to do but inevitably need to. Quitting a job you hate, getting out of a relationship that isn't right, picking up and moving somewhere new, chasing your crazy, half-baked soul dreams despite all logic telling you not to. There will always be reasons not to do it. The cacophony of a million zippers telling you to stay put. You go through all of the unpleasant things that will follow in your mind and you lie around, hoping if you're still enough it'll all just go away. That you won't feel the need to quit, or leave, or chase.

Because what you really want is to have gotten it over with. To be past this place you're in now where things aren't quite right, and as much as you want to "unknow" that, you can't. You don't want to stay here, in this holding pattern. What you really want is to skip over the part where you move from relative comfort to objective discomfort and be at peace. But the only way to get to that place is to wrestle yourself out of the warmth and walk through the sideways sleet.

But in these moments the reality is there is something you need to do and you need to do it. You can lie around and think about how terrible it's going to be and try to wish it away, or you can just get up and do it. Because while you're lying around hoping it will disappear, you are doing yourself no favors. While I tried to wish my pee away, I wasn't out in the cold rain, but I wasn't sleeping either.

You'll try to tell yourself it's not that bad. That you can stand it. That maybe you can work it out somehow. That whatever it is inside you that's telling you to go can be quieted. That you can handle leaving work every day with a headache and a hole in your heart, that you can stand to be loved by someone less than you deserve, that you can settle for a life that is small.

But you can't. Once it's there, that call, that feeling of needing to do something, it will not go away until it's answered. Until the job is quit. Until the breakup occurs. Until the move is made. Until the crazy soul dream is chased. And as Cheryl Strayed says, you can do it later, or you can do it now. You can lie around trying to avoid it, depriving yourself of sleep, or you can just get the hell out of the tent and pee.

Because at some point later, after the zippers and the rain gear and the cold, wet, night, you will be exactly where you imagined yourself. In that place that is better than the one you left, better than the one you avoided all the unpleasantries to stay in. Relief will wash over you and you will realize you should have done this long ago. That even though for a brief time your life was worse, it is now so much soul-shakingly better, because you sucked it up and did exactly what you always knew you needed to do.

Get up. Brave upsetting the calm. Face what you have been dreading and know you will come out on the other side better for it.

I Am Number One

One of the first things they teach you in a Wilderness First Responder course is how to assess a scene. You've witnessed an accident, or come across the aftermath of one, and you must decide how to proceed. People want to jump wildly into action, to start applying direct pressure or giving chest compressions or doing a head to toe. But in this hastiness to save the patient, to solve the problem, to make everything go back to just being fine, people often make the situation worse.

Paul Petzoldt, the founder of the National Outdoor Leadership School, famously said that before doing anything in an emergency you should sit back and light a cigarette. The mastermind behind the world's foremost outdoor school wasn't literally suggesting his students destroy their lungs, but was rather indicating that rushing into action is not a decision that serves anyone.

And so, in the process of becoming a wilderness first responder, someone who is qualified to respond to an emergency over an hour away from traditional medical care, they teach you the first step of scene assessment: "I Am Number One."

When I was first told this, my immediate thought was that a selfish responder didn't seem like the type I'd want coming to save me. But I Am Number One isn't about being selfish; it's about self-care. It's about ensuring that you, as the rescuer, are in the most effective position to handle the situation and help the people who need it. It's about securing the best possible outcome for everyone involved. And that can't happen if you are compromised.

A classic scenario in which I Am Number One comes heavily into play is an avalanche. Avalanche rescue is a highly time-sensitive endeavor, and the instinct to jump into action is understandable. But if the rescuer is entering terrain that has just proven to be unstable, the number of patients could quickly increase, and the number of rescuers decrease – by one. So the responder must care for themselves before they are able to effectively do anything else.

And so it is – everything must begin with ourselves.

When we are young, we are taught how to treat others. How to be kind to them, how to respect them, how to think of their feelings. We are taught how to speak to others, how to act toward others, how to let others know we care. We are taught how to do all these important things, but often there is something missing in this education that prevents us from having the kind of relationships with others that we desire.

We are not always taught to love ourselves. Or how to do it.

We are not always taught how to speak to ourselves, how to act toward ourselves, how to respect and be kind to ourselves. We are not always taught that every relationship we will ever have will be a reflection of our relationship with ourselves. And if people fully understood that, don't you think they would pour all of their time and effort into caring for the health of that relationship? If you are about to enter avalanche terrain, don't you think you would pause to ascertain your own safety first?

When I was 13 years old, I decided I was fat. I decided my stomach wasn't flat enough and my hips were too wide and my back wasn't bony enough. That the gap between my thighs wasn't big enough and my jawline wasn't defined enough and my arms weren't slender enough. As I was, I did not deserve love. I did not deserve respect. As I was, I was not enough.

So for years I starved myself and exercised myself into the ground, but most destructively I told myself I was a monster. I told myself I was hideous and shameful and flawed. I spoke to myself in ways I would never speak to another person. I showed a complete lack of understanding of how to love and appreciate yourself.

If you walk around your life with a sign on your heart that says, "I am unworthy of love and respect," people will believe you.

If you walk around as this watered-down version of yourself, you will yield results from life that are less than what you're capable of. You'll walk into an emergency situation and realize you don't have your med kit or forget how to do CPR or become rendered useless by an avoidable injury. You must, must, must take care of yourself first.

I walked around the world with this sign on my heart and I received back exactly what you would expect. I was loved by people who, in the end, didn't think I was enough. Who in the end would leave, or balk at commitment. Who failed to comprehend the brilliant shard of the universe I was, just as I had.

I had not paused; I had not heeded I Am Number One. I had tried to jump headlong into a situation that would guarantee me the love and affirmation and acceptance I craved *from an external source* – from another person. And before fully loving myself, I had tried to love someone else. I expected them to love me in the way I wanted, rather than the way I was telling them to. And I'd been caught in avalanche after avalanche. The glimmering miracle of my humanity had been buried, hidden from the world.

So much of what we seek externally demonstrates a lack of that thing within ourselves. We look for love, acceptance, affirmation and security to come from other people, because we fail to provide those things for ourselves.

Someone who loves themselves, accepts themselves, respects themselves and celebrates themselves is a responder who is well educated, full of energy, equipped with the proper gear, possessing a calm, orderly disposition, and in safe terrain. A responder who is fully prepared to execute a successful rescue, who recognizes that caring for themselves first *is* actually caring for others. That being your full, nourished, best self and acting from that place is actually the best gift you can give to the world.

When I was 19 years old, I reached out for help. I recognized I had entered avalanche terrain and I stepped back. I looked around and realized I wasn't where I wanted to be. I spent three years taking the L into Chicago every week to talk to a therapist who would help me create an entirely different life, an entirely different self.

I would emerge from these three years as a woman born anew, as someone who did not starve herself, or exercise herself into the ground to look a certain way, or speak disrespectfully to her body. I started to recognize my body for the marvel it was, started to appreciate it for all the things it allowed me to do. I walked out of my therapist's office for the last time with the sun on my face, feeling like I'd finally cracked the code. I'd finally figured out why my life hadn't been going the way I wanted it to. I had assessed the scene and I was ready to act.

What I realized nearly seven years later, as I clawed my way toward the light after a second heart-shattering breakup, was that I had assessed the scene, I had made sure I wasn't in danger, but I had still failed to make sure I was in condition to respond. I was dehydrated, I lacked the necessary energy to do a multi-mile litter carry and I'd failed to restock crucial items in my med kit. I was in a better position than I'd started out in, but I was still not ready to show up in the fullness of who I actually was.

Though I'd stopped shaming my body for what it was, I hadn't been able to shake the conviction that I wasn't enough. The fear that nobody would ever decide on me. The deep-seated panic that I would always be alone.

If you walk around with a sign on your heart that says, "I am unworthy of love and respect," people will believe you.

So yet again I found myself in a moment that required me to step back. That required me to fight the urge to want to jump headlong into action. That required me to assess my own needs and how I could meet them myself before trying to do just about anything else.

I Am Number One. The mantra from which all other good things naturally come. Going slow to go fast. Taking a few moments to gather yourself before acting, to save them later during the action. Smoking Paul Petzoldt's proverbial cigarette in order to be most effective when it counts.

I could jump into another relationship to attempt to patch the hole I felt in myself, or I could wait, letting opportunities pass by that didn't serve my highest self, and slowly, carefully, start to fill the hole on my own. And when that hole is already full, the scene before you begins to change. You see things you didn't see before, you become aware of options you might have missed, things seem to slow down and you feel fully equipped to act as you need to in order to assure the best outcome for everyone involved.

We are all here, we are all alive, we all have bodies that allow us to run and dance and sing and hug other people. We all have brains and hearts and souls and hopes and dreams and thoughts and questions and answers. We are all tiny, integral parts of this patchwork universe. We are all enough. Always.

If you walk around with a sign on your heart that says, "I am worthy of love and respect," people will believe you.

When I was 26, I led a trip of 13 teenagers around Northern California for two weeks. One hot July day in Yosemite National Park, we hiked on a short, flat trail to Mirror Pond to go for a swim. I hiked in the middle of the pack, the med kit slung around my shoulder, talking to a few of my students.

Suddenly, I heard my name being shouted from behind me and turned around to see another student running up the trail toward me at full bent. A student had fainted behind us on the trail and fallen. It was the last thing you wanted to hear as the person in charge of a group of kids, but it was suddenly my reality.

I sprinted down the trail toward where she had fallen,

protocols and procedures running through my head as I went. *Assess the scene. Check ABC's. AVPU. A&O questions. Head to toe.*

When I arrived, I saw Emilie lying on the ground with her eyes closed, questionably conscious. I determined the scene to be safe. I took two deep, centering breaths, slowing the whirring of my brain just a little. I had another student stabilize her neck in case of injury, and after saying her name, pressing lightly on her arm and watching her eyes flutter open, determined her to be alert. *What's your name? Where are you? What day is it? What happened?*

Even in a moment of emergency, I had taken a few seconds to assess the scene, to breathe into my center, to review my training in my head. I had arrived ready to respond to the best of my ability. I had ensured that I Was Number One, and been able to provide the best care. I had shown up as the fullest iteration of myself.

You're Right

"You're a monster."

I had just broken trail for several hundred vertical feet up to a col in the Arrowsmith Range in New Zealand and could think of no greater compliment.

My NOLS instructor Jared was shaking his head at me. I beamed, the orange light of the advancing dawn nothing in comparison to that which had just been lit within. I felt seen, felt the truth of who I was showing itself to the world.

We'd woken up in the dark and pulled on frozen socks and boots, packed up camp and headed up the mountain with our headlamps lighting the way. We'd spent the previous few days stuck at base camp in a drainage, waiting for a weather window, and it had finally arrived. We'd taken turns breaking trail, and my turn had come last, in the final push to the top of the col.

I'd felt strong kicking steps through the snow, putting my head down and settling into a steady rhythm. I hadn't even realized the rest of the group was well behind me until I'd reached the top and looked back. There was something that happened when I was pushing my body, some sort of flow state I tapped into that I couldn't explain, that felt like the essence of being alive. To move and keep moving was something I intrinsically knew I could do.

It was not the first time my ability to endure had been commented on. Little observations here and there had piled up for my whole life. My mom declaring I was going to be a long-distance runner after my first track meet when I was 8, praise from my friends' parents on my ability to haul up and down the field all game as a midfielder, my ski coach's excitement after I'd scored for the team our first race my freshman year. These words stacked up on top of each other little by little over time until they were tall.

This is actually just straight-up science. It has been named the Pygmalion effect, and it is based on the idea that what a teacher believes about a student's ability, whether or not it is actually true, affects how that student performs. Because, ultimately, in those early stages of development, what adults think about us often dictates what we think about ourselves. And what we think about ourselves dictates how we show up, how we perform. Henry Ford, a man who believed himself to be capable of inventing an automobile, despite copious failed attempts that indicated otherwise, famously said that whether you think you can or you think you can't, you're right.

And so it was for me: a cycle that was difficult to locate the origin of. I showed up to endurance opportunities confident and prepared to perform and received feedback confirming my performance and boosting my confidence. I felt I would be successful and so I was.

And before long, a story had been written, had taken root in my heart and my legs, a story that said I was a girl with a motor; that I could endure. I had a little bit of natural ability, perhaps, but more than anything, I believed the story, and therefore fulfilled the prophecy.

The stories we tell ourselves, and the ones others tell us, create our reality. They can feel like truth without us ever realizing they are merely something we decided to believe. People told me I was fast, that I was strong, so I felt fast and strong. It doesn't so much matter whether or not the story is true, but whether or not we believe it. If we believe it, we live into it.

I lived hard into the story that I was an endurance athlete. I started hiking fast and far, then trail running, then ultrarunning, and with each anecdotal confirmation, the story's skin became thicker, came to feel exactly like fact.

I wasn't good at endurance because I was. I was good because I'd decided to be, because I believed I was. It wasn't wrong, but it wasn't random either.

* * *

I registered for the Grand Traverse having done only one short skimo race three years prior. It was the kind of race that attracted professional athletes, people in spandex who spent their entire seasons traveling to suffer uphill, and then people who have been told they are good at endurance their whole lives and think they can pull something like this off, despite never having done anything like it before.

Despite the fact this was essentially like having skied one run on the magic carpet and deciding to try my hand at expert, hike-to terrain right away, I didn't hesitate to jump on the opportunity to race when it came up. I'd run ultras, I'd been skiing for my entire life, I'd been touring for four years. This was the kind of thing I did, even if I'd never done anything exactly like it. The many layers of my endurance story buoyed my confidence in the fact that in five months I would train and be prepared to complete this race.

This is what stories do – they bridge the gap between what you have done and what you think you can do in a way that can range from necessary to fairly inadvisable. I had the confidence to sign up for a race that was well outside of my experience level, and that confidence was the leap to being able to do it that I needed. It turned out I was fit enough, that I had the endurance, that I was right to think it was something I could do. But I never would have gotten past just imagining it as a possibility if my story hadn't told me I could do it. I thought I could do it, so I could. It was that simple.

So often, we don't even let ourselves get there. We decide we can't do something before we even try, before we even take the first step in that direction. *I can't ski 40 miles overnight in the backcountry, because I don't have the right gear or enough experience and that would be insane.* Two people with the same exact ability level could end up in completely different places because one has the confidence to take a step forward and the other does not.

It becomes more about what we think we can do than what we can do, with what we will allow ourselves to try rather than what we have any business doing.

* * *

There was another story I told myself, one that hadn't shown up until my mid-20s that, like most stories, became more and more true to me each time I told it. I was afraid of exposure, of terrain with consequences. I avoided ski lines that required an exposed bootpack or skin track, I felt my entire body go wobbly when I hiked or ran near the edge of a drop-off. I began to say it like it was a fact: I'm not good with exposure. And the more I said it, the more it felt true. Then when I was presented with an opportunity to be in an exposed situation, I approached it with trepidation, with dread, with certainty it would be a negative experience.

It was a story I'd started telling myself when I was 25, after a harrowing fall skinning in the Alaskan backcountry that had left me rattled. My fingers had curled into claws instinctively and dug into the slushy snow, and I had stopped. I wouldn't realize I'd drawn blood until later, when I was finally able to release my grip on the earth. The sensation of slipping on a ridge where I knew my margin for error was narrow and sliding for a few seconds before I self-arrested was one that haunted me every time I entered exposed terrain afterward. My brain began to erase all the times before when I'd felt confident and proficient with exposure, and the story of falling came rushing to the forefront each time. The sensation of losing control, of moving in a way I hadn't planned, seemed to eclipse any other story I had regarding exposure, a sort of selective amnesia.

I remembered the sensation of sliding down snow on a narrow ridge in Alaska, but I forgot all of the moments that had come before that dared to question the validity of my story. I forgot kicking steps into a hanging snowfield without any traction and feeling tired but undeterred by the consequence that lay below me. I forgot scree skiing, giddy and free, down thousands of feet of terrain. I forgot clambering up class 3 scrambles without a second thought on 14ers. I forgot all the moments that would poke holes in this new fear to hide behind. I forgot all of the stories that would have forced me to be big instead of keeping me small.

Just like the story that told me I was an endurance athlete, this one grew stronger and more three-dimensional with time, until I found myself identifying as the kind of person who avoided exposure. Until I found myself backing off ski lines, avoiding knife-edge ridges and losing trust in my own capabilities in the mountains. Until I found myself unable to make the leap.

I ran and skied and hiked because it was fun, and being afraid wasn't fun. So for a while, instead of pushing into the fear, instead of seeing where it came from and what it was made of, I simply surrendered to it, letting it fold me down at the corners.

I carried my skis through a bootpack in the Jackson Hole sidecountry, trembling with fear on a sketchy 20-foot section with significant drop-offs on either side. I sat at the bottom of a sun-soaked basin, watching my friend Eddie ski a line I'd skipped because of the approach. I sat there wondering why I was like this, wondering why I was the kind of person who couldn't handle exposure.

What I didn't wonder was why I believed it, why I had accepted this story despite so many obvious discrepancies. I just sat in the snow and wished I were different, without realizing all I needed to do to be different was decide to be. Was to decide to believe a different story.

Years after falling in Alaska, I found myself facing a class 3 scramble on the Continental Divide with a full pack. My legs felt wobbly underneath me. I became dizzy as my eyes registered how far it was to fall. I instantly resisted the terrain. I instantly shrank back into my fear-of-exposure story. It felt comfortable and true.

We backed off the ridge, descending thousands of feet and climbing back up to avoid the narrow section of rock that felt like it was asking for trouble. I was discouraged and small and not like myself.

On our route back to the divide, we traveled in an ascending traverse up a steep talus field, and I found myself leaping from rock to rock with confidence and precision, sure of myself.

It occurred to me then that none of the moves I was executing was significantly different from those I'd faced on the knife-edge, and yet my experience of them was nothing alike.

It was the simple difference between risk and consequence. The risk of moving through either type of terrain was nearly identical. The size of the rocks, the type of steps required, the slope angle: they were all comparable. It was the consequence that set the experiences apart. On the knife-edge, one false move would likely result in a fall with irrevocable consequences, and in the scree field a fall might mean scraped-up knees and elbows. Though the likelihood of either of these things happening was the same, the difference in consequence completely altered the way I moved. Objectively speaking, there was no reason I shouldn't be able to successfully traverse a narrow ridge. It was the difference between what I could do and what I thought I could do. My body believed the story, and I moved like a completely different person.

That night I lay awake in my tent and started to see cracks in the story for the first time. What if this had nothing to do with ability and everything to do with mindset? What if I moved confidently instead of fearfully? What if I decided to believe something entirely different?

Two days later, we were preparing for a ridge traverse that would involve similar terrain to what we had faced two days prior, only without the option to skirt around it via a lower route. We would have to commit in order to follow the divide to our southern terminus.

I woke up in the dark that morning to boil water for coffee and decided to tell a new story. I decided to take the endurance story, the one that told me I was capable and skilled and prepared, and insert "exposure" where "endurance" used to be. I was the queen of exposure. I thrived in exposed terrain. I was not only confident about my ability to successfully handle the ridge traverse, but I was excited about it.

All morning I channeled confident energy into my body by imagining myself dropping into one of my favorite ski lines. I felt the eager anticipation, the absolute certainty in my ability to perform, the strength in my legs. I imagined the cold air on my nose, the soft snow beneath my skis. I felt the stoke, the ready-to-charge mentality sink in. I played it over and over again in my head until I actually *felt* the confidence, not just imagined it. I felt the confidence to leap.

So by the time we arrived at the notch in question, massive voids on both sides, my body had been tricked into thinking it was doing something it did well and loved doing.

My story had been that my body shut down when I was in exposed terrain, and it had. I'd been shaky and suddenly questioned and overthought moves I never would have otherwise.

But now my body buzzed with the confidence of the imagined ski line, and it seemed that, despite what I had told myself, my mind had had control the entire time. My body had shut down in the past because my mind had essentially told it to, had backed it into a corner and convinced it that it had no other choice.

As we approached the narrow ridge, I felt an excitement I didn't recognize. I wanted to see if it had worked, wanted to see how I felt with the excited energy of an imagined ski line charging through my body. In exposed terrain, it had always been focused on the consequences rather than the actual moves it would take. My eyes would wander to the drop-off and I'd feel vertigo, I'd want to turn back.

But now I dialed in on the rock below me and nothing else. I narrowed the frame, I ignored the empty space on either side and thought only of where I'd put my feet and hands next.

And I cruised through terrain that would have previously turned me into a shaky, panicky mess. I was still cautious, I was still safe, but my body felt strong, my hand and foot placement felt confident. The experience was transformed.

It happened again a few weeks later as I bootpacked up a couloir. We had our ice axes out and reached a crux move that required us to cross a rock band. I would have to place my axe and put full trust in it to be able to swing my legs up onto the small spine and across the rocks, a move I previously would have backed off from. I had an out – I could have easily transitioned and skied from there, but I looked up at the couloir above me and felt a fierce determination ignite. I wanted to ski down that thing, and so I would have to go up it. I swung my axe into the snow, assured I had a solid point of contact, and swung my leg up, bracing my foot on a rock, and pushed upward until I was able to place my other foot safely.

I paid attention to my body, to how it felt, and there was no weakness, no nervousness, just an unfamiliar drive to keep pushing forward. The instability had curled up like smoke in a candle recently put out, spiraling up into the sky, becoming fainter and fainter with each passing moment.

Each success, each moment I was in exposed terrain and did not fall, seemed to map itself onto the experiences that made me afraid. I found myself not even having to push past anything – it just felt wholly different. The confidence, the fire I'd felt in other moments came flooding back – a repressed memory. Moments flickered past – ascending a glacial peak at sunrise, giggling as I boot-skied down a snowfield while mountaineering, scrambling across exposed ridgelines.

Imagine what you would be capable of achieving if you merely allowed yourself to try. If you had the courage and the confidence to take the leap. If you allowed yourself to believe a story that focused on what you could do rather than what you couldn't. Imagine what might be out there waiting for you, all within reach.

The Tiny Miraculous

I woke up just as the light through my tent walls was shifting from full moonlight to the pale shades of dawn. I pulled on my beanie, stuffed my sleeping bag under my arm and walked out into the morning, following a footpath down to the lake near camp. I nestled myself into a nook backed up against a rock and waited.

I watched everything closely, all the details of what was happening around me. The bird that kept swooping low over the water, tilting its tiny body as it flew. The fish splashing to the surface, creating ripples that began as a messy movement of water, and that became perfect spheres as they radiated out farther and farther into the lake. I looked at the plants and flowers that had made their homes on the shore, tucked into dirt patches between rocks. My eyes ran over the pine trees in the distance, tall and stoic. For a long stretch of minutes, I found myself immersed in only what I could hear and see and feel in my immediate surroundings.

The wispy clouds in the sky began to turn pink, bits of late summer color seeping into the horizon in the distance. The sunrise was imminent. I trained my eyes on the spot in the east I was sure I was about to watch the sun pop out of, any minute now. I stopped paying attention to the beautiful minutiae around me and focused only on the spot I was certain the sun was hiding just behind.

Minutes passed and still nothing appeared. No patch of warm light, no bright orb emerging behind the ridge. The pink began to fade from the clouds, the ambient light growing stronger. It looked like daytime, but still nothing. Where was the goddamn sun?

I found myself distracted from all the things that had held me wholly captivated before. Frustration began to boil up. I had woken up early to watch the sunrise before returning to camp and cooking breakfast with my friends. I had sought out some solo nature meditation, something that always brought me peace and joy. I was waiting for my mind-blowing, life-affirming mountain sunrise, and instead there was nothing. Rather than continuing to focus on what *was* before me and waiting patiently, knowing the sun would eventually come up, as it always did, I became fixated on the fact that it wasn't here yet and what the fuck.

We do this to ourselves all the time. We obsess over the things in our lives that haven't materialized yet, and in the process miss all of the things that are already here. And all the energy that is spent feeling frustrated that certain things haven't turned up protracts the entire process. It is focusing our energy on what we don't have, rather than smothering it all over what we do have.

We all want things and are working toward them. We may feel like we have done everything in our power to manifest those things, and feel confused and disappointed that they are still nowhere to be found. Haven't we shown up, stated what we wanted from the universe, put in the work and waited patiently? Don't we deserve to be reaping the benefits of our dedication? Where the hell is the job or the human or the recognition or the success? Give us the goddamn sunrise already!

I spent nearly 30 minutes this way, picking my split ends and thinking about the mountain bike ride I'd be going on later, rather than paying any attention to the nature I'd woken up early to sit and look at. And so I lost twice. Not only was I not watching the sun rise over the ridge but I wasn't watching any of the wonderful things that were already there either. In my fixation on what wasn't yet there, I was missing what was.

My experience had begun to revolve around the outcome, rather than the process. As the moments dragged on, all I wanted to see was the sun coming up over the ridge, the moment I thought would contain the highest beauty. I no longer cared about the subtle changes occurring in the light with each passing second, was no longer able to appreciate each stage for its particular beauty. I wanted only the outcome, only the sun popping up on the horizon.

If we are in it for the outcome, the process becomes a chore. The process becomes something we begrudge and bemoan and wish would just be over already. And yet, in most cases, the process is 90 percent of the experience and the outcome maybe 10 percent. We spend most of the time in the process, and if we can't find wonder and magic in that, we will spend the large majority of our time being pissed off, cranky and missing the point entirely.

After what seemed like an impossibly long time, I saw a ring of light appear from behind the trees in a spot way farther left than where I'd been looking. More northeast than east. It quickly became clear the sun would do this whole thing absolutely whatever way it wanted. It was on no one else's schedule, and had agreed to no one else's rules for where it would appear. It was going to rise, but it was going to do it however and whenever and wherever it damn well pleased.

The sun is always going to rise. Of that we can be infinitely, resolutely certain. And if we view the outcome as an unambiguous *truth*, then there is no point in running mental circles, wondering why it hasn't appeared yet. It will happen when it happens. The sun answers to no one, it rises when it rises, and getting frustrated when it isn't doing it on our self-imposed schedule is utterly pointless.

If we can begin to view the outcome we desire in this same way, as something that is concretely in existence on some future plane, then we can release our attachment and anxiety around it not having appeared yet. It will come, it will be, and in the meantime, we live. We do not squander that which has already appeared worrying about that which has not.

If we really lean into the process, if we love each part of it for exactly what it is, if we realize that everything is happening on the exact schedule it's going to happen on, then we win. We spend the time before the outcome dialed in and enjoying what's around us, and before we know it, the sun is up. Yet it feels different, it feels less critical. It's not what we have centered our energy around. It's merely another beautiful thing to stack on top of the pile of beautiful things we are experiencing and have already experienced. If you learn to love the process, you get to experience 100 percent awesomeness instead of just 10 percent.

A few days later, I jumped at a rare opportunity to take a sunrise run during the week. When I began, light had just started to seep into the sky. The air was cool, belying the eventual heat of the day. The tall dry grass rustled in the wind and there was no one else on the trails. I felt my legs pump under me in a steady rhythm, watched two deer leaping up the hill into the shrubs away from me. The morning was still and quiet in a way it wasn't in the evening, when I usually ran.

I was coming off an injury that had prevented me from running as much as I usually would, and so even getting to spend an hour moving quickly over dirt and rock felt like a miracle. The clouds turned pink to the west, and I could feel the warmth of encroaching light. I took in the sunflowers in clusters on the side of the trail, felt focused on the dance of the decline, the pleasant burn of the incline and, before I knew it, I was cresting an east-facing hill and there was the sun. It had appeared without me waiting for it, as it was always going to do. And when it came, though I savored the pale warmth on my skin and the light draped over the cliffs above me, it was not the main event. It was a part of something larger, something wonderful among many wonderful things, a mere added bonus to the spectacle I was already immersed in. On this morning, I had given myself an hour full of joy and meaning instead of 45 minutes of exasperation and a few minutes of *well-freaking-finally*.

And the best part is we get to choose. We can't make the sun come up any faster than it's going to. We can't dictate where it will vanquish the horizon. But we can decide how we pass the time in between. We can decide to dwell in what's already all around, harboring inside us a calm knowing that the outcome will arrive precisely when it's supposed to. The outcome carries the weight we give it. It can be everything, or it can be one of many things that bring us light.

What we seek is out there, hovering somewhere below the horizon line, not yet seen. But we have to know, we have to believe beyond the slimmest shadow of a doubt, it is there and it is coming. And if we know that, we are in no hurry. If we know that, we can relax and direct our attention elsewhere. If we know that, we are not prisoners of our outcome, resigned to wait until forces beyond our control conjure up what we've asked for. If we know that, we are free.

Acknowledgements

To my parents, Jim and Mary, who have always believed this book would be born even when I didn't, and who have supported me in every way possible to be able to complete it. To my grandparents, Pop-Pop and Pat-Pat, who have been my most unwavering fans from the beginning. To my brothers, Rob and Matt, who have supported me even through their teenage years when they would pretend not to read anything I wrote.

To Hanna Bartels and Emma Longcope, who had first eyes on the original draft of this book and dedicated time to giving me invaluable feedback – I love and am inspired by both of you.

To Sean Prentiss, Lily King and Steph Jagger, who took the time to pay it forward to a young writer in need of advice and direction.

To Liz Fleury, Charlotte Agell, Becky Pride, Nancy Shaw, Deb Johansen and Eula Biss – teachers who nurtured my love for writing and helped me hone my craft.

To Zoe Balaconis, Molly Herber, Gina Begin, Ryan Dunfee, Sean Prentiss, Ben Lester, Manasseh Franklin and Mike

Rogge – editors of visionary publications who believed in my essays from the beginning.

To Maddie Boardman, whose thoughtfulness helped jump-start my career in the world of outdoor writing.

To my therapist, Stacy Clark, whose guidance over the last ten years has allowed me to step into my power and have the mental and emotional space to create this book.

To the late Tyler Lorenzi, who once said to me on the Northwestern University lakefill at dawn that every piece of writing should be a comment. I hope this comment finds you.

To all the incredible adventure partners featured in this book: Justine Cornelison, Colt Horvat, Julianna Lord, Jessica Ferko, Marielle Meurice, Geoff Bell, Julian Astor Asdurian, Sebastian Quezada Alvarado, Lindsay Bourgoine, Nikki Hodgson, Ethan Friedman, Babalu Danger Jones, Ben Kain, Sally McAdam, Julie Highland, Jim Highland, David Rose, Heather Seal, Meghan Quirk, Jared Spaulding, Natalie Taylor, Diego Rojas, Joe Connolly, Emilie Courtot, Eddie Lamair, Lauren Deeley, Sara Higgins and Gabby Makatura – it's been an honor and a privilege getting amongst it together.

To the ancestral lands of the Te Ātiawa o Te Waka-a-Māui, Ngāti Koata, Ngāti Toa Rangatira, Ngāti Kuia, Rangitāne o Wairau, Ute, Cheyenne, Arapaho, Pueblos, Kawashkar, Abenaki, Shoshone, Miwok, Yavapai, Havasupai, Hopi, Squamish, Lil'wat, St'at'imc, Ahtna, Dena'ina, upon which these experiences took place.

Many of these essays have appeared elsewhere prior to being a part of this book, as follows:

"Out Here" was published in the National Outdoor Leadership School's alumni magazine, *The Leader*, in 2013.

"Waking Up in the Wilderness" appeared in the NOLS blog in 2015 and was published in the book *A Worthy Expedition: A History of NOLS*, in 2016.

"What Would You Do with Your Days?" was published in the digital edition of *Misadventures Magazine* in 2015.

"Warmth" was published in the digital edition of *Misadventures Magazine* in 2015.

"Flowing through the Footholds" was published in the digital edition of *Misadventures Magazine* in 2014.

"Legends of the Fall" was published in *Backcountry Magazine* in December 2015.

"Reach" was published on the Teton Gravity Research website in 2015.

"The Things We Carry" was published in *The Leader* in 2013.

"Or" was published in the blog *WildSnow* under the title "A Grand Traverse Gone Awry," in 2019.

"Triangulation" was published in the digital edition of *Misadaventures Magazine* in 2016.

"In the Thick of It" was published under the title "Sometimes the Hardest Part and the Best Part Are the Same," in the digital edition of *Misadventures Magazine* in 2015.

An excerpt from "A Love Letter to Winter" was published in the digital edition of *Misadventures Magazine* in 2017.

"How Can I Support You?" was published under the title "How Can I Support You? The Power of Expedition Behavior," on the NOLS blog in 2017.

"Tolerance for Uncertainty and Adversity" was published on the NOLS blog in 2017.

"For the Love of the Tour" was published in the November 2017 edition of *Backcountry Magazine*.

"Going Alone" was published under the title "Going Solo," in the digital edition of *Misadventures Magazine* in 2015.

"Lean In" was published under the title "Leaning In: Charging Fear and Freshies," on the Teton Gravity Research website in 2015.

"Will You Do It Later, or Will You Do It Now?" was published on the Teton Gravity Research website in 2016.

About the Author

Writer, teacher and lover of sufferfests, Carolyn Highland always goes the extra mile in search of wild metaphors that provide insight into life's tangliest quagmires. Over 50 of Carolyn's essays have appeared in publications such as *Backcountry Magazine*, *The Ski Journal*, *Misadventures Magazine*, *The Leader*, the Teton Gravity Research and WildSnow websites, among others. Carolyn's writing has also been used in course readers for the National Outdoor Leadership School (NOLS), the Prescott College Outdoor Program, the Second Nature Wilderness Program and NatureBridge. Carolyn received a BA in creative nonfiction writing from Northwestern University in 2012.

Based in Truckee, California, Carolyn spends every spare second backcountry skiing, trail running, backpacking, mountain biking and rock climbing. When not getting after it outside and writing about it, Carolyn can be found teaching fourth graders at Tahoe Expedition Academy how to write an excellent paragraph, handle their emotions responsibly, be anti-racist and poop in the woods.